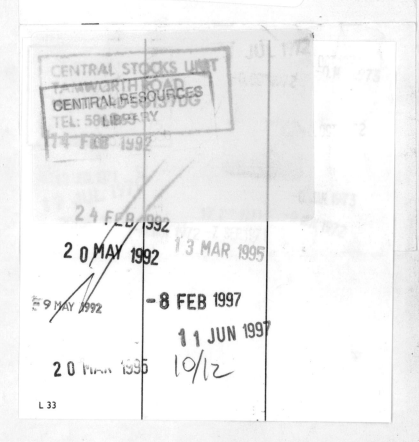

TYNESIDE POTTERY

Lithograph by Hawkins of painting by
J. W. Carmichael, 'Ouseburn Viaduct'.
A pottery chimney is seen through the
large arch on the left. (L.A.G.)

TYNESIDE POTTERY

R.C. Bell

Photography
by
Michael Plomer

Studio Vista

Produced by November Books Limited, 23–9 Emerald Street, London WC1N 3QL.

Published by Studio Vista Limited, Blue Star House, Highgate Hill, London, N19.

Text set by The Lancashire Typesetting Company, Bolton, Lancashire.

Printed by Taylor Garnett Evans and Company Limited, Greycaine Road, Bushey Mill Lane, Watford, Herts.

Bound by Dorstel Press Limited, West Road, Templefields, Harlow, Essex.

© *November Books Limited 1971.*

SBN 289.70053.1

Designer: Thomas Carter.
House editor: Celia Phillips.

The author is indebted for help in the preparation of this book to many individuals and organisations, so many that there is fear of unintentional omission. Great courtesy was shown by the Chief Librarian and staff of the Newcastle City Library; the Gosforth Public Library; the Central Library of Newcastle University; and the Public Libraries of North Shields, South Shields, and Sunderland. The Newcastle booksellers, T. Pickard, and R. D. Steedman, were also most helpful.

Specimens of pottery were lent for study and recording by the Laing Art Gallery, Newcastle; the Shipley Art Gallery, Gateshead; Mrs M. Bell of Tynemouth; Mr R. Bolam, Newcastle; Mr H. Bell, East Hartford; Mr A. H. Adams, Stocksfield; and Mr C. T. Maling, Gosforth.

Help in the search for Tyneside pieces was given by several antique dealers, including Ian A. Robertson, N. Jewett, N. McDonald, Margaret Maughan, O. Humble, E. Hattam, Jean Trench, and Dorothy Rowe. The Dunlop Rubber Company provided the photograph of the Durham China Company. Adamsez Ltd. permitted reproduction of photographs from an early catalogue. Mr John Potter provided useful information about Sheriff Hill Pottery.

Especial thanks are due to Hoults Ltd. for permitting the study of the material in Maling's last pattern shed; and to Dr Margaret Gill for her drawings of the impressed marks and photographs of the printed ones—an exacting and time-consuming task.

Finally to my wife and family who have shared our home for so long with a motley collection of pots!

Major firms
Readers will note that nearly half the illustrations are of pieces produced by Maling firms. This is a reflection of their relative importance in the area, both in size and length of operation. Most Tyneside firms were small and only existed for a few years; their pieces are scarce and are exciting acquisitions for collectors. Only the potteries at St Peter's, St Anthony's, North Shields, Sheriff Hill, and Stepney approached the Maling firms in importance. The highest quality early pieces came from St Anthony's and St Peter's.

Abbreviations
L.A.G.—Laing Art Gallery, Newcastle upon Tyne; S.A.G.—Shipley Art Gallery, Gateshead; M.L.S.—Maling's last shed; M.B.—Mrs Margaret Bell, Tynemouth; R.B.—Mr R. Bolam, Newcastle.

Method of mark notation
M—numbers refer to impressed marks; I—numbers refer to incised marks; m—numbers refer to printed marks; p—numbers refer to painted marks (see pp. 137–146).

Other works by the same author:
Board and Table Games from Many Civilizations, Vols. I and II
'Board and Tile Games' in *Encyclopaedia Britannica*
Tangram Teasers
Commercial Coins 1787–1804
Copper Commercial Coins 1811–1819
Specious Tokens and those struck for General Circulation
Tradesmen's Tickets and Private Tokens 1785–1819

Contents

Part One

Introduction

The once flourishing earthenware industry of Tyneside began with the establishment of a pottery for making brown-ware by Mr John Warburton at Pandon Dean about 1730. Some 20 years later he transferred his business to a new pottery at Warburton Place, Carr's Hill, near Gateshead, which was the first to produce white earthenware in the north of England. The main portion of this pottery closed in 1817, though a small part of the building remained in use for making brown-ware as late as 1892.

Between 1780 and 1790, three important potteries were built at St Anthony's, Stepney Bank, and Ouseburn. A pottery at North Shields followed in 1814, and in 1817 the factories of Thomas Fell at St Peter's and Robert Maling at Ouseburn Bridge began production; other potteries soon followed. In 1827, Parsons and White stated that there were about 20 potteries on the banks of the Tyne. Flints and potters' clay were brought as ballast in colliers returning from the south of England, while the chief materials used for colouring and glazing were procured locally. There was abundant coal near at hand, and merchant vessels using the Tyne were available for transporting the potters' wares to countries throughout the world.

W. Parsons and W. White, *History Directory and Gazette of the Counties of Durham and Northumberland*, volume I 1827; volume II, 1828.

In the second half of the 19th century there were fewer pottery firms in the area, but those that remained grew in size and efficiency, and employed a greater total number of workers.

In 1863 C. T. Maling wrote that at that time six firms on Tyneside manufactured white and printed wares, four white-printed and brown-ware, and three brown-ware only. Together they employed some 1,200 hands, using 12,000 tons of white clay and 3,000 tons of brown, the Ford Pottery supplying at least 80 per cent of the jam and marmalade jars used in England and Scotland. By 1863 none of the raw materials

C. T Maling, *The Industrial Resources of the Three Northern Rivers, The Tyne, Wear and Tees*, 1863, 2nd edition 1864.

used in making common earthenware were obtained in the neighbourhood, but came as ballast in ships visiting the port.

Collingwood Bruce, in 1863, described the manufacture of earthenware at that time.

Potter's clay, a soft plastic mud resulting from the disintegration of former rocks, possesses the property of being easily moulded into any form; and on being exposed to heat, loses its plastic nature, hardens, and retains its shape. Clay as it is dug from the earth in Dorsetshire, on being burnt, shrinks so much and is so liable to crack in cooling, that before being employed in the potteries is submitted to previous treatment to correct this, as well as to free it from impurity.

The rough clay is mixed with water to an extent which reduces it to the consistency of thick cream, thus separating the stony and grosser particles from the finer.

Flints, previously heated red hot and then thrown into water to render them friable, are ground in water under heavy stones, and produce a liquid resembling that obtained from the clay. A small quantity of Cornish stone, which is a partially decomposed feldspar, is ground with water, and some China clay added to improve the colour. This admixture deprives the clay itself from the tendency to shrink, and also confers strength. The whole is passed through extremely fine sieves, only the finest particles being allowed to proceed. Iron impurities cause yellow, reddish, or black stains on the ware; hence the liquid tlay or 'slip' passes a series of magnets, which attract nearly all the ferruginous particles, and eliminate the stains caused by their presence in the native clay. The slip is run into large hearths of fire-clay ware, and surrounded by an edge to retain the liquid in the 'slip pan'. Heat from below expels the water until the resulting mass attains suitable consistency. After being well worked up so as to have the clay solid and uniform in texture, it is ready for the potter.

A skilful 'thrower' takes a chunk of clay, guessing the quantity with extraordinary accuracy, dashes it on a horizontal revolving disc, and moulds it into shape with great speed. A good workman can turn out 3,500 to 4,000 bowls or cups in a day's work of $10\frac{1}{2}$ hours. As the articles leave the thrower's hands they are soft and easily lose their shape. To avoid this they are carried away on boards by children, into stoves where they are partially dried, sufficiently to bear being turned on a lathe, where the outsides are turned down with great speed to the exact shape.

The ware is then placed in 'saggars', or vessels of fire-clay; and multitudes of these, so filled, are set in a large cone, or kiln; heated by means of several fires placed round its exterior. The saggars preserve the shape of the ware, and at the same time prevent contamination by smoke and impurities in the fire. After 50 hours' firing the ware is removed as *biscuit*. The biscuit is then dipped in a finely ground creamy glaze previously fused from a mixture in which borax and white lead, ground flint, etc., form the chief ingredients. After this the ware is placed again in saggars in the glost kiln, and in 15 to 17 hours is drawn as ordinary white or '*cream-coloured ware*', by which latter name it is known in the market.

In manufacturing printed ware the pattern is printed on tissue paper, which is immediately laid on the biscuit. The porous nature of the ware absorbs the oil, and with it the colouring matter so retentively, that on plunging the different articles into water, by moderate friction the paper is removed, leaving the printed pattern adhering to the ware. Exposure to a low heat burns off the oil, after which it is immersed in the glaze, as before, and fired in the glost kiln—the vitrification of the glaze permitting the pattern being seen underneath.

Common painting is done by hand, and in other respects the subsequent treatment is the same as when printed ware has to be produced. To some extent machinery has superseded the labour of the thrower in certain articles in large demand.

Besides ordinary 'thrown' articles, many goods are made by flattening the clay out, and pressing it into forms of plaster of Paris. Plates are made in this way, and on one occasion 12,000 dozen were received as one order by a pottery on Tyneside.

Collingwood Bruce, *Hand-book to New-castle-on-Tyne*, 1863.

The above account requires some enlargement. Earthenware is clay hardened by the action of fire. It is opaque, granular in texture, and when unglazed permeable to water. Clays differ in character; some are 'short' and difficult to work, others are plastic, easily manipulated, and retain shape when modelled or thrown on a wheel, or cast as liquid slip in a plaster-of-Paris mould.

Red clays are generally more plastic than white. Some clays shrink more during firing from rapid evaporation of free moisture, a tendency reduced by the addition of pulverised fragments of fired pottery, or *grog*.

Earthenware ranges in colour from white through a variety of hues to strong reds and browns, the colour being due either to chemical impurities in the clay, or to the addition of colouring matter. The whiteness of clays is increased by the addition of calcined flints, a discovery made about 1720.

In the smaller brown-ware potteries primitive earthenware was made of local clay unmixed with other ingredients. It was damped and shovelled into a *pugmill* where it was chopped and minced by knife blades, and then forced through a small hole as a solid rod and cut into convenient lengths with a wire. It was then *rolled* and *wedged* to make it plastic for the potter's wheel. The potter halved his lump of clay, slamming one piece down hard on top of the other, then rolled the two pieces together with a kneading action, and cut the lump in half again. He continued this process until the clay became rubbery, and then threw it onto the centre of his potter's wheel which was driven by a foot treadle.

As the piece of clay revolved the potter's hands hollowed it out into the desired form; with a variety of tools he shaped its foot, and inscribed any desired bands, finally smoothing the sides with a fine damp sponge. He then cut the vessel from the wheel with a wire, and set it on a drying rack to harden.

When hard and dry the vessels were placed in saggars and stacked in the biscuit kiln. When the latter was full the opening was bricked up; fires lighted beneath were kept stoked for 48 hours (maintaining a temperature of approximately 1200°C) and then allowed to go out. About three days later the kiln was unbricked and emptied. The ware in its biscuit state was hard, brittle, and porous like a plant pot. It was then dipped in a liquid glaze, dried and refired in a glost kiln at a lower temperature (approximately 900°C) than the original firing.

Higher quality white-ware was made from a mixture of clays with the addition of china, stone and flints, in careful proportions. After about 1840 traces of iron compounds were removed by passing the fluid slip over powerful electro-magnets. The water was then filtered off from the slip through a filter press, leaving the solid clay behind. This clay contained air bubbles and was treated in a pugmill until it reached suitable plasticity for working.

Many objects were made on a wheel, dried to *leather* hardness, and then turned exactly to size on a lathe and burnished with a steel tool.

In *casting*, slip was poured into plaster-of-Paris moulds made in several parts. The plaster absorbed water, and a layer of clay was deposited against the side of the mould; the surplus slip was poured off, and as the mould dried the clay inside the mould shrank a little and separated from its container. The cast was then wiped with a damp sponge to

Top.
Grinding clay and flints.

Bottom left.
Flint crushing machine.

Bottom right.
Plate-making.

Applying underglaze transfers.

Loading a kiln. Note saggars in right foreground.

A pottery bank.

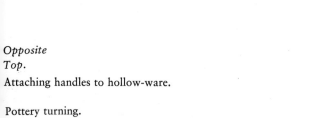

Opposite
Top.
Attaching handles to hollow-ware.

Pottery turning.

Bottom.
Placing items into saggars.

Loading a biscuit-kiln.

remove any traces of seams; cast handles and spouts were added by dipping them in slip and sticking them onto the ware, any surplus being sponged away.

Plates were made on a *jigger*. The potter threw a ball of clay onto a revolving wheel, flattened it, and then threw this pancake over a plaster-of-Paris mould shaped to the upperside of the plate. The mould and clay were then rotated on the jigger and the potter shaped the bottom of the plate with a metal template. The mould and clay were then left to dry, when shrinkage enabled the latter to be lifted, smoothed with a damp sponge, and placed on a rack. When the plate was chalk white and dry it was ready for the biscuit kiln.

Decoration was usually applied in the biscuit state by transfer-printing or hand-painting. The pigments were mixed in an oily emulsion which was volatilised by a light firing, and the ware was then glazed, dried, and fired in a glost kiln. Such *underglaze* decoration was fast to washing and rubbing, being under the glaze, but the range of colours was limited to pigments capable of resisting the great heat of the glost firing.

Overglazing consisted of decoration applied onto the glaze instead of beneath it, and the ware was fired at a lower temperature (about 700°C) in a *muffle* kiln. A wide range of colours was available, but the decoration was liable to wear off with frequent washing or rubbing. Often pieces were decorated with a combination of underglazing and overglazing, the latter being palpable with the tips of the fingers as raised above the general surface of the glaze.

Glazes were glassy compounds applied to biscuit-ware in a liquid form by dipping, and when fired gave a glossy film which was impervious to water. Glazes could be transparent, revealing the colour of the earthenware body or applied pigments beneath; or could be opaque and contain colour themselves.

Decoration may be applied to earthenware in the *green* or *leather* state as slip decoration; in the biscuit state as brush-work or transfer-printing; over the glaze on unfired tin enamel when the colours must be able to withstand glost kiln temperatures; or in enamel colours applied over the fired glazed surface, which is refired at a much lower temperature in a muffle kiln. The range of underglaze pigments is more restricted than that of those used in overglaze decoration, but the underglaze colours are softened by the layer of glaze and are usually more subtle and refined. Underglaze decoration is permanent.

Crazing is due to the unequal contraction of body and glaze resulting in a network of fine cracks. These may occur immediately after cooling, or more commonly after several months or years. Placing glazed earthenware in a cooking oven hastens the process and also causes ugly yellowing or browning. A deliberate crazing known as *crackle* was used extensively by Chinese potters for its decorative effect.

Gilding was first introduced as size-gilding, a process only used for a short period. About 1790, wares were decorated with gold in a solution of mercury, which on firing produced a dull matt finish requiring burnishing. Bright liquid gold was a much later discovery. At first the gilding was done by hand, then by transfer-printing from copper plates carefully engraved to a very shallow depth to save waste of metal. Gold decorations were also applied with rubber stamps, though the result is less clean and exact.

Lithography was first used to decorate earthenware by A. Ducote, who patented the process in November 1839. The design was drawn on lithographic stone in acid-resistant wax, and the background then removed with dilute nitric acid, leaving the details in the decoration standing out in relief. The stone was then inked with potters' varnish and an impression taken upon transfer paper with lithographic size. This was transferred to the surface of glazed pottery and dusted with powdered pigments. Underglaze lithography was performed in the same way, using vegetable gluten instead of potters' size.

Decoration in several colours was obtained by lithographing a stone for each colour, and impressions in varnish taken upon prepared transfer paper. Each successive impression, taken in turn from dark to light, was sprinkled with finely ground enamel and dried before the next application. The colours were metallic oxides. Photo-lithography and other photomechanical processes of reproduction are inventions of the last few years.

Terracotta is biscuit earthenware and ranges in colour, according to the temperature of firing and the type of clay, from soft ochres and chalky pinks to strong purple-reds.

Stone-ware is earthenware, opaque, completely fused and vitrified by firing at very high temperature, and is intensely hard, being resistant to the edge of a steel knife. It is non-porous and does not require glazing, though it is customary to do so when used for tableware.

Traditional manufacturing processes in the pottery industry persisted well on into the 19th century. The first potters' roller-printing machine was introduced in 1833. A plate- and saucer-making machine introduced in 1844 had to be abandoned because of opposition from workers fearing redundancy. Machinery for making pottery was in general use only by about 1870, and automatic pottery equipment is a 20th-century invention.

Most early Newcastle ware was cream-coloured, some being perforated in the Leeds manner. Later, ordinary white earthenware was often ornamented with metallic pink lustre ovals, enclosing various scenes, transfer prints of portraits and marine subjects, or innumerable topical verses, many displaying Rabelasian humour. A popular motif was the High Level Bridge, a quarter of a mile long across the Tyne, completed in June 1849 at a cost of £243,000. Built to carry a railway above a road, it was one of the engineering wonders of the world. The driver of the first train to cross it is said to have remarked to his fireman at the beginning of the journey, 'Weel Geordie mun, 'ere's for 'eaven or Gaitshed [*sic*].'

More than a hundred firms have made earthenware on Tyneside during the last two centuries, but only a handful are mentioned in standard works on English ceramics. Their goods were intended for middle- and working-class homes, and with a few exceptions did not rank with the best work produced in London, Worcester and Staffordshire. Tyneside wares satisfied local needs, and were exported to Denmark, Norway, Germany, the Mediterranean countries, India, and to London for re-export to the colonies and North America.

Tyneside pottery throughout its history simulated wares from other parts of the country; the Geordie potters copied works of Bow, Chelsea, Bristol, Swansea, Staffordshire and Sunderland, and there is little doubt that many unmarked pieces of pottery ascribed to these famous centres originated on the banks of the 'Coaly Tyne'. Most of the raw materials were imported, and therefore there is no characteristic local paste, while many of the potters had learnt their craft elsewhere and styled their products in familiar ways. All collectors of English earthenware need a knowledge of Tyneside pottery to distinguish northern copies from pieces produced by firms further south. 'Leeds cream-ware' was produced in the St Anthony's pottery, 'Gaudy Welsh' from the Tyne Main Pottery, 'Sunderland lustre' from the Ouseburn Bridge Pottery and the Low Lights Pottery, North Shields, and Willow pattern by Maling, Fell, Patterson, Burn, Rogers, and several others. Considerable quantities of unmarked delft-ware in the north-east leaves little doubt that there was a local source of supply, though conclusive evidence is still lacking.

Types of Pottery made on Tyneside

Banded-ware Blue, brown and yellow slips were prepared and poured into a three-sectioned funnel with three separate spouts. Biscuit-ware was then placed in a horizontal lathe, and the potter held the funnel over the revolving earthenware, allowing a fine stream of tri-coloured slip to flow onto it. By manipulating the funnel and speed of the lathe a wide range of bands, spots, curves and spirals could be produced. The ware was then dried, fired and glazed.

Blue-Printed Earthenware Transfer-printing in underglaze blue was introduced into the north-east by the Maling brothers at the Hylton Pot-works on the Wear. The design was engraved on a copper plate which was warmed and colour suspended in oil was worked into the design. All surplus colour was wiped off, and a piece of tissue paper dampened with soap and water laid over it. Both were passed through rollers of a press, and then the copper plate was heated to allow the paper to be removed without tearing. The pattern was then trimmed and applied to the ware in biscuit state and rubbed with a stiff brush to press the design into the surface of the ware. The latter was placed in water; the paper soaked off, and the printed design left ready for firing to a temperature high enough to volatilise the oil and leave the pigment behind. The ware was then dipped into glaze and fired in a glost kiln.

By the end of the 18th century romantic Chinese scenery, exemplified by the Willow pattern, had been joined by equally romantic English scenery of castles, cathedrals, cottages and Highland cattle. Classical ruins in Italy were depicted, tiger hunts with elephants for the Indian market, and views of the cities of the New World for America, while famous faces stared out from frames of floral and foliate borders, or elaborate surrounds of shells, scrolling, vignettes, animals, portraits, and landscapes.

There was a phenomenal rise in blue-print decoration between 1820 and 1840, and coinciding with it the use of marks consisting of the name of the pattern, and the initials or title of the manufacturer within a cartouche or scroll.

The invention of transfer-printing was a milestone in ceramic history; permitting the quick duplication of craftsmen's designs by semi-skilled labour. Black outlines speeded additional hand-colouring, and by the middle of the 19th century earthenware was covered with complicated multi-coloured decorations with additional gilding.

The depth of the blue depended upon the purity of the cobalt used,

A copper plate for printing transfers belonging to Robert Maling, *c.* 1820. The engraver was Adam Buck, b. 1775, d. 1833. (L.A.G.)

15

Underglaze transfer. Willow pattern tea cups in biscuit state, with transfer paper applied, and after removal of paper. (C. T. Maling & Sons). (L.A.G.)

Overglaze transfer. Plain white glazed cup, cup with transfer applied; and cup after transfer removed. (C. T. Maling & Sons). (L.A.G.)

Sewell & Co. M118. Cream-ware filigree basket and stand. (L.A.G.)

Opposite.
Top.
(*left*) silver lustre resist-ware jug: (*centre*) silver lustre cream jug: (*right*) copper lustre resist-ware jug with enamel decoration. These pieces are all unmarked but probably made on Tyneside. (L.A.G.)
Bottom.
C. T. Maling & Sons. Rington tea jars showing (*left to right*) local bridges, cathedrals, and castles. Marked m84, and a variant.

16

Opposite.
Top.
(*left*) Joseph Sewell. Quintal pink lustre
flower holder, marked M114. (L.A.G.)
(*right*) Collingwood & Beall. Pink lustre-
ware jug. (L.A.G.)
Bottom.
(*left*) Thomas Patterson. Pink lustre
cottage plate, marked M102.
(*right*) Sewell. Pink and white saucer,
marked M114. (L.A.G.)

and ranged from clear light blue to nearly violet. Before 1800 light blue
was preferred; at the turn of the century dark blue became fashionable;
around 1830 light blue regained popularity, only to lose favour again
about 1880.

Cream-ware Most cream-ware was left plain, relying for its appeal on
good modelling and cut or pierced designs. The latter were achieved by
piercing the soft, unfired clay with metal tools, a process made quicker
by Wedgwood, who introduced dies to cut part or the whole of a pattern at
once.

Figures Throughout the 19th century many figures were made from
local red clays. Slip was poured into plaster-of-Paris moulds, the moulds
absorbed water and a uniform layer of firm clay formed. Surplus slip was
then poured away and the mould with its contents placed in a dryer.
While drying the earthenware contracted and the shape could be lifted
from the mould. In this way large thin-walled hollow figures could be
made cheaply; until the middle of the century figures were usually in the
round; later flat-backed pieces became common. Overglaze enamels
were used for colouring, chiefly red, green, yellow, and black. All had a
tendency to flake from the glaze when thickly applied.

Dogs formed an important part of the figure-maker's stock-in-trade,
used to decorate shelves and mantlepieces in cottage and middle-class
homes. Representatives of almost every breed may be found. Spaniels
were the most popular, closely followed by greyhounds and whippets,
sometimes holding a newly killed hare in their mouths. Other sporting
dogs included pointers standing over game, setters with 'feathers'
streaming in the wind; curly-haired foxhounds in full cry; harriers,
staghounds and springers. The coaching Dalmatian hound and the pug
also appeared. The 'Comforter' or spaniel's gentle, a lap dog bred
from the Maltese terrier crossed with King Charles' spaniel, was a
favourite. Pottery comforters were made in pairs to face each other
across a mantlepiece, and were in five sizes, ranging in height from 6 to
18 inches.

Between 1840 and 1865 enormous numbers of full-length figures of
celebrities were made; royalty, military and naval heroes, politicians,
preachers, jockeys, actors and actresses, lined the potters' shelves.
Unfortunately pottery figures are rarely marked, and none seen by the
author have been identifiable as being made on Tyneside. However, at
least two local potters, John Bagshaw and James Hollingshead, are
known to have made figures, and as there are considerable numbers of
these 'Staffordshire' pieces in homes and antique shops in the area many
were probably produced locally. Confirmation by finding a marked piece
is still awaited.

Lustre-ware Lustre is a thin deposit of metal on pottery giving a metallic
or iridescent sheen. Unfortunately the term is used for two very different
decorative effects.

Originally an attempt was made to imitate gold and silver vessels by
precipitating the salts of gold and platinum onto earthenware, but the
thickness of the pottery made such pieces clumsy, and the venture met
with only partial success. Lustre was best used in conjunction with
moulding, painting or printing.

Copper lustre was the commonest, the colour varying with the salt
used, and the kind of clay beneath, every tone of copper, bronze and gold
being possible. The best copper lustre applied to thinly potted ware has a
smooth surface, especially inside the foot-rim, distinguishing it from the
grittiness and irregularity of many modern reproductions. The cheapest
pieces had no other decoration, monotony being avoided by yellowish-
buff bands of unlustred earthenware. Others had bands or panels masked
from lustre, and these white surfaces were then painted with enamel,

See *Resist-ware*, p. 20.

covered with transfer printing, or decorated with plain or mottled pink lustre.

Some lustre-ware has over-painting on the lustred surface, usually in strong reds, greens or blues, or on moulded reliefs forming vine patterns, garden flowers and hunting scenes. Silver lustre, obtained with platinum salts, was used for teapots, cream jugs, slop-basins, and vases of all descriptions, as a cheaper imitation of costly silver originals. Lustre was also used as an alternative to gilding, or in broad bands around the rims and bases of black printed jugs, and sometimes to frame enamelled decorations. Usually the bodies of these lustred pieces were left white, but occasionally they were painted yellow or blue. Such items are now rare and valuable.

Gold salts suitably diluted were also used to produce a range of pinks and purples having a characteristic metallic sheen, but not simulating a metal. Mottled and marbled washes, sometimes referred to as 'tear stains', appeared on jugs, bowls, and mugs, in conjunction with doggerel verse, black printed views of bridges, ships, harvest scenes and masonic emblems. Similar printed ornaments and lettering were used on purple-lustre wall-plaques, bearing religious texts inspired by the preaching of John Wesley and his followers. Most of these pieces are ascribed to Sunderland, though many unmarked items were probably made on Tyneside.

Mocha-ware William Evans described this method of decoration as the effect produced by letting fall a drop of '... a saturated infusion of tobacco in stale urine and turpentine, and it ramifies into the resemblance of trees, shrubs, etc.'

The process was used from about 1780 until 1914. The earliest dated example, now in the Christchurch Mansion Museum, Ipswich, is lettered 'M. CLARK, 1799'. Mocha-ware was mainly used for ale, shrimp, and nut measures, and occasionally for kitchen and table wares. In the pottery trade it was sometimes known as 'Tobacco-spit ware'.

Early mocha decoration occurs on cream-ware bodies, but from the 1830s white earthenware or a hard cane-coloured stoneware was used. Shades of brown, green or yellow were applied to the biscuit-ware, and over this a pigment was applied, usually brown but sometimes blue, green or black, mixed with tobacco and hop extract, which acted as a diffusing agent and created patterns suggestive of trees, feathers or moss.

Mugs and jugs for taverns from 1824 onwards bear an excise mark applied by the Weights and Measures Office. Considerable quantities of this ware were made in north-east England from 1810 until about 1890.

Resist-ware A decoration of flowers, birds, animals, leaves or other design was painted on biscuit-ware with a soluble solution, sugar being commonly used. After dipping in lustre, the sugar was washed away, leaving the design unlustred. Alternatively the design could be lustred, and the rest of the area protected. Occasionally silver-resist wares were sparingly decorated with enamels.

Sponge-ware Pigment from an impregnated sponge was applied to cheap glazed earthenware. The colours were shades of blue, pink, green, brown, purple and an occasional dash of yellow. Sponging might be in monochrome or polychrome, and applied as stippling, bands, splotches or swirls. It was also used in conjunction with hand-painting—flowers, fruits, houses and birds being common motifs. Sponging was occasionally combined with transfer-printing.

Akin to sponge-ware was rubber-stamp-ware, designs being stamped onto biscuit-ware before the latter was dipped into glaze.

Tortoise-shell-ware This was cream-coloured earthenware enriched with semi-translucent glazes producing mottled patterns in brown, green, and blue, from the use of oxides of manganese, copper, and cobalt.

Mocha-ware bearing official stamps of Edward VII. Unmarked pieces. (M.L.S.)

See p. 99.

William Evans, *Art and History of the Potting Business*, 1846.

Stamped ware, unmarked. (M.L.S.)

See p. 21, Maling pint and half-pint mugs stamped with an excise mark of Edward VII.

See p. 17.

See p. 17.

Registration Marks

Until 1842 there was no protection against piracy of ceramic designs or shapes. In 1840 a committee of Members of Parliament issued a 600-page report advocating comprehensive copyright of industrial designs, and an act of Parliament in 1841 provided copyright on ceramic and glass designs for three years. By law all protected articles were required to bear the letters 'Rd' for registered, and code letters and numbers corresponding with the date of registration. See p.24.

From 1843 until 1867 the year was shown by the letter in the top inside corner of a diamond, the other three inner corners indicating the month of issue on the left, the day of issue on the right, and the parcel number identifying the manufacturer at the bottom. In 1868 a new arrangement was introduced as every letter of the alphabet had been used. The top compartment represented the day of issue, the parcel number was on the left; the year on the right; and the month at the bottom. See p.24.

Years						Months	
1842	X	1856	L	1870	C	January	C
1843	H	1857	K	1871	A	or	O
1844	C	1858	B	1872	I	February	G
1845	A	1859	M	1873	F	March	W
1846	I	1860	Z	1874	U	April	H
1847	F	1861	R	1875	S	May	E
1848	U	1862	O	1876	V	June	M
1849	S	1863	G	1877	P	July	I
1850	V	1864	N	1878	D	August	R
1851	P	1865	W	1879	Y	September	D
1852	D	1866	Q	1880	J	October	B
1853	Y	1867	T	1881	E	November	K
1854	J	1868	X	1882	L	December	A
1855	E	1869	H	1883	K		

Eccentricities

See G. A. Godden, *Encylopaedia of British Pottery and Porcelain Marks*, 196.

For September 1857 from 1–19 September the symbol 'R' was used; for December 1860, 'K' was used; for 1–6 March 1878 the incorrect registration mark, W, was used instead of D.

The diamond device is found both printed or impressed (and moulded). Printed marks usually refer to the added decoration, and impressed or moulded marks to the shape of the item.

In January 1884 registered designs were numbered consecutively with the prefix 'Rd' or 'Rd. No.'.

Rd. No.	reg. in	Rd. No.	reg. in
1	Jan. 1884	1	Jan. 1884
19754	1885	291241	1897
40480	1886	311658	1898
64520	1887	331707	1899
90483	1888	351202	1900
116648	1889	368154	1901
141273	1890	385500*	1902
163767	1891	402500*	1903
185713	1892	420000*	1904
205240	1893	447000*	1905
224720	1894	471000*	1906
246975	1895	494000*	1907
268392	1896	515500*	1908
*Approximate numbers only		550000*	1909

Sculptured work could be registered at Stationer's Hall, thus securing freedom from copying for 15 years under the act of 21 June 1798. Some stoneware mugs and jugs ornamented in high relief were included as sculptured work, and have inscribed on their undersurface: PUBLISHED BY (with the maker's name and address, and the date). A copyright model required the maker's signature and the date of publication. Infringement of copyright entailed damages and costs against the guilty party.

Imperfect marks

Potters were paid by piece work, and tended to rush the seemingly unimportant marking of pieces. Printed marks may be smudged and illegible, and impressed marks blundered or incomplete, making recognition difficult unless the perfect mark is known to the examiner.

The rare stag's head mark of John Carr and Sons is illustrated, as is an incomplete marking depicting part of the stag's head, half the buckler with the words '& SONS' and part of the anchor. The stamp had been pressed unevenly into the soft clay, but enough of the pattern is present for firm identification of this piece of 'Sunderland lustre' (it was sold as such) as being made in North Shields.

The same stag's head mark of John Carr & Sons is also shown with the head missing. The anchor and part of the lettering can be made out, and this incomplete mark served to identify the printed mark associated with it, which previously has not been recorded. Two marks on the underside of a Willow pattern side plate are illustrated. The impression would suggest that the firm had tried to sell its wares as 'made in Staffordshire', and the 'J.C. & Co' intended to be mistaken for Joseph Clementson. The stag's head impressed mark, M25, however, is unmistakeable. The author has another Willow pattern side plate with the same printed mark but without the tell-tale impressed one.

Although imperfect marks may give valuable information, they can also lead to false identification. Anchor devices were used by several firms on Tyneside, and confusion may arise with blundered or imperfect impressions. Porcelain firms also used an anchor, including the Bow Porcelain Works, Anchor Porcelain Company, Chelsea and Chelsea-Derby, Coalport, Davenport, Derby and Worcester. Porcelain pieces should not cause any difficulties, but some of these firms also made earthenware pieces marked with an anchor, and anchor devices were used in Europe and America.

Diagrams of registration marks of the first and second series.

YEAR — CLASS — IV — DAY OF MONTH — MONTH — R^D — PARCEL NUMBER

1868–1883

DAY OF MONTH — CLASS — IV — YEAR — PARCEL NUMBER — R^D — MONTH

1842–1867

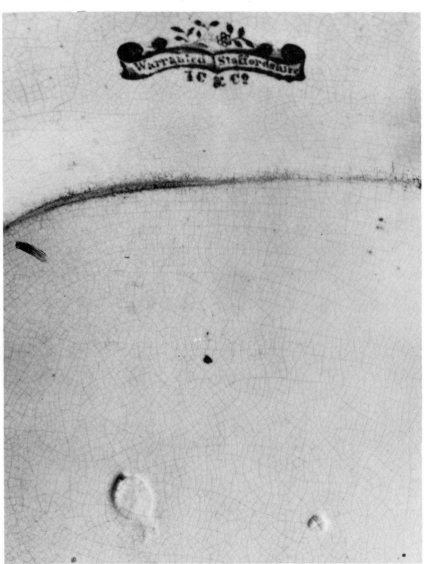

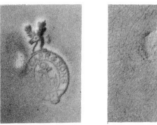

Imperfect marks of John Carr & Sons.

The earthenware products of Thomas Morris, P. Stephen, J. Woodward, The Middlesboro' Pottery Company, and Thomas Patterson can be easily confused.

The author has seen pieces made by T. Morris, and the Middlesboro' Pottery Company on display in a museum as products of Thomas Fell.

The Patterson anchor mark is shown on page 145, and if the impression is not clear the Fell and Patterson marks are easily confused. The Middlesboro' mark may be confused with Carr & Sons mark with the stag's head missing.

Recognition of Tyneside Pottery

Known Tyneside pottery marks are indexed on pages 138 to 146 of this work, but there are others yet to be discovered, and for collectors who have to decide whether a particular piece was made on Tyneside or elsewhere the following points are helpful:

(1) Only earthenware was made on Tyneside, and any piece of porcelain may be disregarded. The sole exception to this rule was the Durham China Company, which produced feldspar china.

(2) Staffordshire pieces often bear the initial of one of the seven leading pottery towns in the county:

B	Burslem	L	Longton, also Lane End
C	Cobridge	S	Stoke-on-Trent
F	Fenton	T	Tunstall
H	Hanley, incorporating Shelton		

(3) A Staffordshire knot indicates origin in this county. It first appeared about 1845, and was very popular in the 1870s and 1880s. Compare the mark of Bodley and Co. with the mark of Burns and Co., Newcastle.

Marks of (*top to bottom*) Thomas Morris, P. Stephen, J. Woodward, The Middlesboro' Pottery Company, and Thomas Patterson.

Mark of Bodley & Co., Scotia Pottery, Burslem.

Aids in Dating Pieces of Earthenware

Earliest date

See Godden, op. cit.

1800   Printed marks came into general use about 1800, though used on porcelain decorated with underglaze blue patterns as early as 1760.

1800   An item bearing any printed mark incorporating the Royal Arms, or version of the Arms was made after 1800.

1801   Royal Arms with an escutcheon and surmounted by a cap of Maintenance indicates a date between 1801 and 1814.

1810   An item with any printed mark incorporating the name of the pattern was made after 1810.

1814   Royal Arms with an escutcheon and surmounted by a crown were used between 1814 and 1837.

1837   Royal Arms without an escutcheon were used after 1837.

1840   The garter mark was used extensively from 1840 onwards.

1840   The term 'STONE WARE' only occurs after about 1840.

1843   Diamond registration marks began in 1843, and can be dated to the exact day of the month.

1850   The word 'ROYAL' in the manufacturer's title or in the trade name suggests a date after 1850.

1855   'LIMITED' or 'LD' or 'LTD.' after a firm's title indicates manufacture after 1855, and was not in general use until 1880.

1862   The word 'TRADE-MARK' signifies a date after the Trademark Act of 1862, and usually a date after 1875.

1884   'Rd. No.' followed by a number signifies a registration date after 1883. Design registration began on 1 January 1884. The article itself may, of course, have been made several years later. If the number is above 360000 the date is after 1900.

1891   'ENGLAND' was added to marks in 1891 to comply with the American McKinley Tariff Act.

1900   'MADE IN ENGLAND' signifies a date after 1900.

Tyneside Potteries and their Proprietors in Chronological Order

This list is compiled from many sources, including contemporary trade directories, the latter printed from handwritten lists, sometimes badly written. Alternative spellings thus occur, e.g. 'Patton' and 'Patten'. It may be difficult at times to decide whether two individuals are listed, or whether there are two spellings of the same name.

Pandon Dean
c. 1730   John Warburton (brown-ware).

Skinnerburn, also known as the Newcastle Pottery and Forth Banks
ante 1736   Joseph Blenkinsop & Ralph Harl.
1748   Advertised in local papers to let.
1758   Burnt down.
1787   George Spearman & Co.
1790   Addison, Falconer & Co.
1824   Addison & Co.
1827–9   Taylor & Son.
1833–8   Redhead Wilson & Co.
1837–8   Thomas Wallace & Co.
1838–58   James Wallace & Co.
1858–93   Wallace & Co. Closed in 1893 when Wallace & Co. moved to Foundry Lane, Ouseburn.

Carr's Hill, also known as Warburton's Place
c. 1740–95   John Warburton.
1795–1811   Isaac Warburton.
1811–17   Ellen Warburton. In 1817 the main portion of the pottery closed. A small portion remained open for brown-ware.
1827–38   Thomas Wallace & Co. In 1838 they transferred to Skinnerburn.
1844–51   Kendall & Walker.
1847   Benjamin Parker.
1851–5   M. Kendall.
1867   Isaac Fell & Co. Transferred to South Shields in 1871.
1873–5   Lowry & Hardy.
1877–82   T. Hardy.
1883–4   J. Hopper.

1885–8	Thomas Patterson. Moved to St Anthony's.
1889–90	Patterson & Parkinson. Moved to St Anthony's.
1891–2	Patterson & Scott. The pottery seems to have closed the following year.

Newburn Pottery
| 1749 | John Brougham. |

Heworth Common Pottery
| 1757 | Mentioned in local papers. |
| 1760 | Up for sale. |

Heworth Shore Pottery (probably the same as the above; there seems to have been at least two small potteries present some of the time)
1795	Put up for sale by Thomas Sill.
1822	Mr Wood.
1827–37	Joseph Wood. Probably the same person as above. He was also a grocer.
1827	Thomas Codling.
1828	Jacob Dawson.
1828	John Codling.
1833	Joseph Warburton.
1833–8	Patterson, Dawson & Codling.

Hebburn Quay Pottery
| 1757 | Up for letting. |

Tyne South Shore Pot-house
| 1757 | Mr Hillcoat. He was still there in 1769. |

Acomb Pottery
| 1764 | John Lee. |

Sheriff Hill Pottery
ante 1773	Paul Jackson.
1787–97	William & C. F. Jackson.
1798	Jackson & Co. Probably sold before 1811.
1824	J. Fordy & Co.
1827	Fordy & Patterson.
1833–8	Jackson & Patterson.
1837	John Ferry.
1837	Patterson & Co.
1844	Patterson & Codling.
1847	Thomas Patterson.
1851–92	George Patterson.
1892–5	Marshall King (from North Shields).
1895–1902	Robinson, Gray & Burns: trading as the Sheriff Hill Pottery Company Ltd. Robinson died in 1902.
1902–6	Gray & Burns. Gray died in 1906.
1906–9	Burns died in 1909 and the factory closed.

According to Jewitt, writing in 1878, Lewins & Parsons occupied Sheriff Hill at one stage.

Sheriff Hill, or Gateshead Fell (two names for the same place – about 2 miles south of Gateshead) is called Sheriff Hill because the sheriff, mayor and corporation of Newcastle met the judges of assize at this spot in order to conduct them to Newcastle; the old London Road goes through this village (Gateshead Fell).

Ouseburn Pottery
1782	Smith, Harvey & Co.
1786	Backhouse, Hillcoat & Co.
1790	Hillcoat, Brown & Backhouse.

1801	Robert Yellowley.
?1821–3	H. Elliott & Co.
?1824	James Tuer & Co.
1827–37	T. & J. Thompson.
1837–64	John Maling. The pottery was called the Old Pottery, Ouseburn in a directory of 1858.
1841	Turpin & Co. mentioned in a directory of 1841.

St Anthony's Pottery (1)
ante 1784	James King & Co.
1787–95	Chatto & Griffiths.
1795	William Huntley.
1800	Foster & Cutter.
1804	Joseph Sewell.
1819	Sewell & Donkin.
1852	Sewell & Co. The firm closed in 1878.

There seems to have been a small brown-ware pottery in the same district. A directory of 1837 mentions William Wilson; and there is another reference in 1858 to J. Gibson.

1882–4	W. Lloyd.
1885–6	Lloyd & Hodges.
1891–2	Patterson & Parkinson.
1892	T. Patterson & Co. The works closed in 1808.

New Pottery, Ouseburn (Stepney Bank Pottery)
1786	Dale & Head.
1791	Head & Dalton.
1811–16	John Dalton & Son. It was then renamed the Stepney Bank Pottery.
c. 1816	Dryden, Coxon & Basket.
1821–3	John Dryden & Co. This firm then seems to have moved temporarily to St Peter's, presumably while the new Phoenix pottery was being built.
1824–33	Davies, Cookson & Wilson.
1833–44	Dalton & Burn.
1844	John Harrison.
1847–52	Thomas Bell & Co.
1852–60	J. Burn & Co.
1861–75	John Charlton. The old pottery was removed to make way for a bridge. The New Stepney Pottery was built and opened in 1877 (see below).

Tyne or South Shields Pottery
ante 1790	Mentioned in local papers.
1830	Mr William Robertson.
1841–67	John Armstrong & Co.
1871–*c.* 1890	Isaac Fell & Co.

The Northumberland Pottery,
North Shields (later known as the Low Lights Pottery)
1814	?Collingwood & Beall.
1821–3	Bird & Co.
1829	Cornfoot, Colville & Co.
c. 1832	Cornfoot, Patten & Co.
1834	Cornfoot, Carr & Patten.
1847	Carr & Patton.
1848	John Carr.
c. 1850	J. Carr & Co.

1854   J. Carr & Son.
1861–1900 J. Carr & Sons. The firm ceased to manufacture pottery in 1900, though continued to make fire-bricks.

Ballast Hills Pottery, Ouseburn
1824–33 E. & R. Wilson.
1837   William Wilson (brown-ware).
1844   John Tate.
1850–60 J. Hollingshead (a figure maker).

Ouseburn Bridge Pottery (later the Albion Pottery)
1817   Robert Maling.
1853   C. T. Maling.
1860   Bell Bros. Renamed the Albion Pottery
c. 1863 Isaac Bell, Galloway & Atkinson.
c. 1864 Galloway & Atkinson.
1865–70 W. Atkinson.
1871–5   W. Morris.
c. 1876 Pottery closed.

St Peter's Pottery
1817   Thomas Bell & Thomas Fell, trading as Fell & Co.
1827   Thomas Fell & Co. (John Dryden and H. Barker seem to have worked there for some time as well.)
1837   Frederick Russell (stoneware) seems to have been at North Shore, and worked at Fell's pottery, or very near it.
1890   Pottery closed.

Tyne Pottery, Felling Shore
1821–3 Tyler & Co.
1827   Taylor, T. & Co. (Moved to Newcastle Pottery in 1827.)
1827   Joseph Wood.
1827–9 Thomas Patterson.
1833   Codling & Co.
1837   Patterson & Co. This is probably the same T. Patterson as at Sheriff Hill in 1847.
1861–2 J. Kirton & Co.

Folly Wharf, Sandgate
1824   Brameld & Co.
1827–9 Smith & Co.
1837   John Wood.
1847   Robert Wilson.

Walker Pottery
1824   George Armstrong.

Phoenix Pottery
1827   John Dryden & Co. (Transferred from New Pottery, Ouseburn via St Peter's.)
1844   Isaac Bell.
1847   Carr & Patton.
1857–8 Phoenix Pottery Co.
1858–9 Bell, Cook & Co.
1860   Factory converted into a chemical works.

Old Customs House Quay, North Shields
1827   Aaron Lees.

Tyne Main Pottery, Salt Meadows, South Shore
1831–44   Richard Davies & Co.
1844–51   R. C. Wilson.
1852–3   D. McGregor.

Ouseburn Flint Mill
1837–8   Ralph Charlton.

Lime Street Potteries (Nos. 5, 7 and 9 Lime Street)
When known the street numbers are given.
1837–54   J. Bagshaw. In 1854 he moved to 25 Cut Bank.
1844   Taylor Booth.
1844–51   Ralph Davison.
1855–60   C. Walker, 7 Lime Street.
1865–6   J. Sampsou, 9 Lime Street.
1865–8   C. W. Fenwick, 7 Lime Street.
1869–70   T. R. Leighton, 7 Lime Street.
1870–2   Gardener, 7 Lime Street.
1873–4   Mould & Stonehouse.
1877   W. Laing.
1877–85   E. Hutchinson, 5 & 7 Lime Street.
1887–8   J. Young.
1888–98   J. R. Forster, 5 & 7 Lime Street.
1898–1900 Burnside Bros., 5 Lime Street.
1902–3   Wallace & Co., 7 Lime Street.

Arthur's Hill
1844   H. Rawling, William Street, Arthur's Hill.

Railway Bridge Pottery
1844–53   John Charlton ⎤ possibly working in the same building but
1847–51   George Gray ⎦   as separate firms.
1852–7   Morrow & Parke ⎤ possibly working in the same building
1857–8   Mr Rogers   ⎦   but as separate firms.
1858–60   W. Blakey.
1860–80   Robert Martin & Co.

Cut Bank Pottery
1854–5   John Bagshaw. (Moved from neighbouring Lime Street.)
1857–8   Robert Hall.
1859–64   J. Cooper.
1863–4   J. Forster.

Jarrow Brownware Pottery
1851   G. Grey & Co.
1852–3   J. B. Hodgson.

Stepney Square Pottery
1851–8   J. Holmes.

St Laurence
1855   Humble & Morris.

Ford Pottery (Old Ford Pottery) (A)
1859   C. T. Maling. Renamed Old Ford Pottery in 1879 when the
            New Ford Pottery (B) was built at Walker.

Stepney Street Pottery
1863–75   G. R. Turnbull. Address given variously as 16 or 14 Stepney
            Street.

Crawford Row, Ouseburn
1863–75   John Charlton. May have been a relation of the earlier
            John Charlton at the Railway Bridge Pottery.

Pottery Lane, Ouseburn
1865–77   J. H. Walker. He then transferred to Foundry Lane.

Charlotte Street, South Shields
1874–5   G. S. Young.

KEY TO MAP SHOWING SITES OF POTTERIES

The potteries are numbered from west to east, irrespective of when they
were built or demolished, and range in time from John Warburton's
brown-ware pot-house built about 1730 at Pandon Dean, to the Durham
China Company's factory erected in 1951 on the Team Valley Trading
Estate. Many changes have occurred in the names and positions of streets
over the period, and therefore only a few modern main roads are indicated
together with the Tyne, Team and Ouseburn rivers.

   Potteries showing floor plans are accurately placed; those indicated by
a circle are only sited approximately.

1   Adamsez, Scotswood
2   Durham China Company, Team Valley Trading Estate
3   Skinnerburn Pottery, Forth Banks
4   Pandon Dean
5   St Anthony's Pottery (2), Argyl Street
6   Sheriff Hill Pottery
7   Carr's Hill Pottery, Warburton Place
8   Stepney Bank Pottery
9   Flint Mill
10 Cut-Bank Pottery
11 Lime Street Potteries
12 Railway Bridge Pottery
13 Phoenix Pottery
14 Ouseburn Pottery (Old Pottery, Ouseburn of J. Maling)
15 Ouseburn Bridge Pottery
16 Ford (A) Pottery
17 Tyne Main Pottery
18 Ford (B) Pottery
19 St Peter's Pottery
20 Friars Goose
21 Felling Shore Pottery
22 St Anthony's Pottery (1)
23 Heworth Shore Pottery

Map of Tyneside potteries.

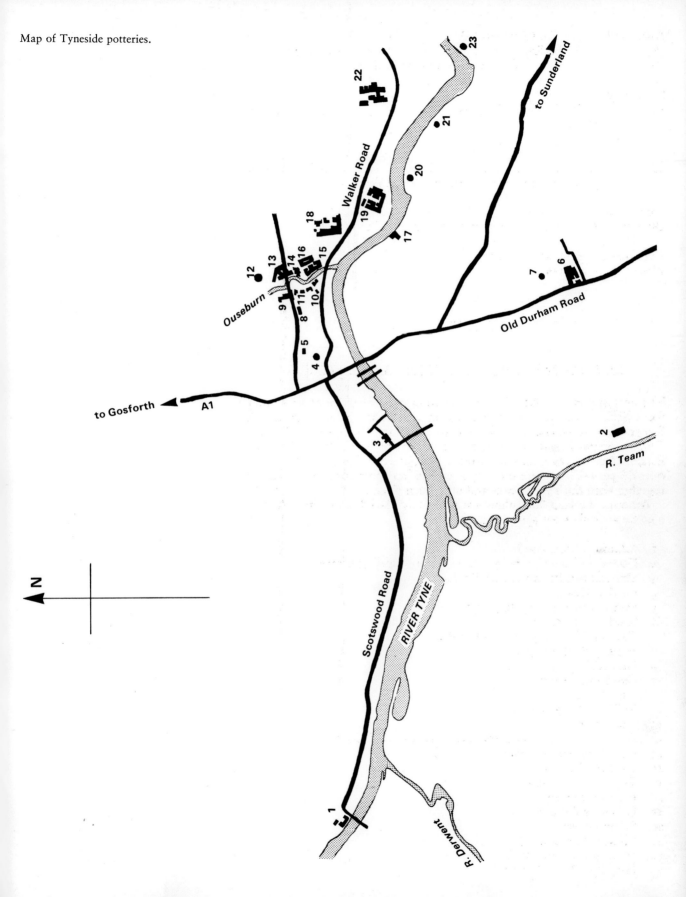

New Stepney Pottery

1877–1912 John Wood & Co. They transferred from the old Stepney Bank Pottery when this was demolished to make way for a bridge.

Foundry Lane

1879–86　John Hedley Walker. He seems to have transferred from Pottery Lane in 1879.

1883–92　Cuthbert Kendle Walker.

1893–4　Wallace & Co.

New Ford Pottery, Walker (B)

1879　C. T. Maling.

1890　C. T. Maling & Sons.

1947　C. T. Maling & Sons (Hoults Ltd).

1963　The pottery closed in July of this year.

Gateshead Art Pottery

1884　Gateshead Art Pottery Co., East Street, Gateshead.

Pipewellgate Pottery, Gateshead

1896–1909

Scotswood

1902　Adamsez Ltd. began production of Adamesk pottery.

1920　Adamsez Ltd. began production of Elan pottery. This is still being made.

Prudhoe Pottery

c. 1910

St Anthony's Pottery (2)

1949　Nixon & Bolam.

1951　Moved to Argyl Street.

1955　Pottery closed.

Durham China Pottery, Earlsway, Team Valley Trading Estate

1950　Durham China Company.

1954　Pottery closed.

A directory of 1855 records a James Schofield, Ouseburn Pottery. It has not been possible to discover which pottery he occupied.

Earthenware Dealers

A few dealers sold wares back-marked with their own names, and these may cause confusion with earthenware manufacturers. Three marks have been found, and there may be others. Two examples are illustrated. See also Addendum, p. 149.

Opposite.
(*left*) Adamsez. Adamesk jar marked M2. (L.A.G.)
(*right*) Adamsez. Elanware bat jar marked M4. (L.A.G.)

Two back-stamped pieces with china dealers' names. These were not earthenware manufacturers.

The Townsend mark occurs on a Queen Victoria Jubilee mug dated 1897. Note the late use of the word 'semi-porcelain', which is usually considered to indicate pieces made during the early years of the 19th century. Two further china-dealers are known to have backstamped their wares: F. J. Cullen, Newcastle, and Cullen & Son, Newcastle on Tyne. Their marks are not illustrated.

Opposite.
(*left*) Fell & Co. A coloured transfer decorated lustre jug with a bramble design, marked m51. (*right*) Fell & Co. A hand-painted lustre-ware jug, marked m52, and dated 1874.

Watercolour by
J. W. Carmichael,
'Mr Reay's Flint Mill'.
(L.A.G.)

38

Part Two

An Alphabetical Arrangement
of Pottery Proprietors
and their Factories

Adamsez Ltd. (Formerly Adams & Co.)
Scotswood-on-Tyne

About 1840 a Mr Gibson started a brick and tile works at Scotswood-on-Tyne, using local clay. In 1880 the works of W. C. Gibson & Co. Ltd. were taken over by the Adams twin brothers, as Adams & Co., and fire-clay was used for making sanitary ware. Fire-clay is found beneath coal seams, originally having been the soil in which the primæval forests grew, and then subjected to great pressure and heat in geological times. The Adamsez's coal mine and clay pit at Scotswood is illustrated. From it they obtain clay and coal for use in the factory.

In 1904, Mr Moses J. Adams began the manufacture of 'Adamesk' Art Pottery, made of fire-clay and covered with a leadless glaze. The smaller pieces were used for internal decoration, and the larger for garden ornamentation: bird-baths, plant and fern pots and vases; cemetery urns, and church baptismal fonts. A few pieces of Adamesk were unmarked, but most bear the monogram MJA, or ADAMESK impressed.

A. B. Searle was a member of the firm at this time, and many of the feldspathic glazes used were invented by him. One of these glazes contained 45% feldspar, 25% flint, and oxides of zinc, barium and calcium as whitening. The colours were obtained by the addition of metallic salts: green produced by copper salts; blue by cobalt salts; yellow by titanium salts; bronze by manganese and copper salts.

The Adamesk pottery was fired in an old-fashioned muffle-kiln at 1200°C, and the long period of heat produced subtle plays of colour not obtainable with the quicker tunnel-kilns of today. An analysis of one of the glazes carried out by Mr Bernard Moore in 1916 showed:

silica	50.76%	lime (CaO)	5.30%
alumina and		potash (KO)	3.40%
ferric oxide	11.50%	soda (NaO)	2.30%
lead oxide	nil	loss when calcined	
zinc oxide	8.53%	over 100°C	7.28%
tin oxide	5.29%	sulphur	
magnesia	0.03%	trioxide (SO)	2.22%
barium oxide	3.26%	carbon dioxide	
		(CO)	2.97%

About 25% of grog (ground-up pottery) was added to the raw clay from the mine. Two of the recipes for earthenware bodies were:

Body A
ball clay 26 parts; china clay 19 parts; flint 11 parts; stone 8 parts; feldspar 8 parts.

Body B
china clay 50 parts; flint 23 parts; feldspar 13 parts; stone 7 parts; ball clay 6 parts.

The production of Adamesk pottery ceased with the outbreak of World War I.

Mr Alan H. Adams joined his father's firm in 1912, and became the director in 1921. He was responsible for most of the firm's modelling, and designed many of the shapes for the world-famous sanitary ware which is outside the scope of this book. He also created the unusual 'Elan' pottery, and the pieces were impressed with his mark, 'M5. (AHA)'. Elanware is still being sold at the Adamsez works, Scotswood. He also designed ornamental tiles, plaques and busts,

and exhibited two years in succession at the Royal Academy. This is the only firm on Tyneside still producing pottery, albeit of fire-clay and not earthenware.

Addison & Co.   *Skinnerburn Pottery*
Forth Banks, Newcastle

Mentioned in a directory of 1824; successors to Addison, Falconer & Co., and followed by Taylor & Son.

Addison, Falconer & Co.   *Newcastle Pottery*
Forth Banks

The pottery was bought from George Spearman & Co. in 1790, and Addison, Falconer & Co. are mentioned in directories of 1790, 1801, 1811, 1821–2, and 1823. By 1824 the firm had become Addison & Co., and the pottery had changed its name to the Skinnerburn Pottery.

The Museum of Practical Geology, London, has a frog mug printed in black, with a monument and trophies in memory of Lord Nelson, and inscribed NEWCASTLE POTTERY. (See Newcastle Pottery, p. 95.)

Armstrong, George
Walker

Mentioned in a directory of 1824 as producing brown-ware.

Armstrong, John, & Co.   *Tyne or South Shields Pottery*
Oyston Street, South Shields

Mentioned in directories of 1844, 1847, 1851–2, and 1853. Mr John Armstrong bought the Tyne or South Shields Pottery in Waterloo Vale from Mr Robertson about 1841. It had been established before 1790, as shown by the following advertisement from the *Chronicle*, 8 May 1790:

> South Shields Pottery to let. A tenant may be accommodated with all utensils now used for carrying on the business, and a convenient warehouse situated near the river. Apply at Mr Fairle's Office, South Shields.

Atkinson, W.   *Albion Pottery*
Ballast Hills, Ouseburn

Mentioned in directories of 1865–6, 1867–8, 1869–70. He succeeded Galloway and Atkinson, and was followed by Mr W. Morris.

Backhouse, Hillcoat & Co.   *Euseburn Pottery*
Ouseburn, Newcastle

Mentioned in a directory of 1787. The *Courant* of 4 November 1786 tells of the beginning of the partnership:

> The intended partnership in carrying on the Euseburn Pottery, and fixed under the firm of Hillcoat, Almack and Co. (but never ratified), is this day entirely at an end. Mr Daniel Almack having declined the Business of a Pottery, the said Euseburn Pottery will in future be carried on under the Firm of Backhouse, Hillcoat and Co.

Two views of Adamsez's factory, Scotswood (1970).

Girls decorating 'Adamesk' leadless glaze artware, c. 1906.

Coal mine at Scotswood owned by Adamsez Ltd.

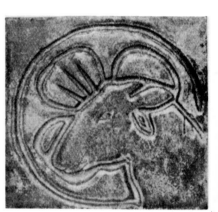

Illustrations from a catalogue published in 1906 (a) an Adamesk tile, (b) a panel, (c) an Adamesk garden flower vase.

c

Illustration from the same catalogue of indoor pieces of Adamesk pottery.

Adamsez four-handled vase of Adamesk pottery (marked M1). (L.A.G.)

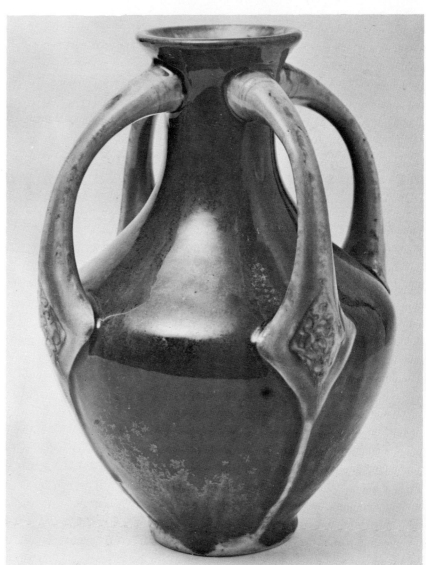

Adamsez jar with handle of Adamesk pottery, marked M1. (L.A.G.)

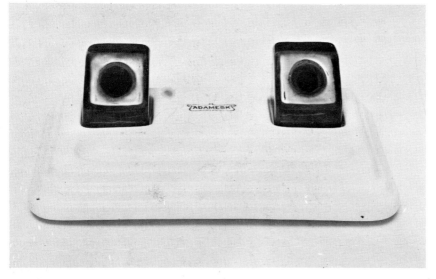

Adamsez. Adamesk ink stand, in deep blue and white.

Adamsez. Elanware, 'the dancer'.   (L.A.G.)

Adamsez. Elanware 'Mother with Child', unmarked but presented by Mr Alan H. Adams.   (L.A.G.)

Tyne or South Shield Pottery. Note TYNE POTTERY on west and east points of the compass on the side of the mug. No mark beneath.   (L.A.G.)

In 1790 the firm had become Hillcoat, Brown & Backhouse, Brown having a half share and being the principal manager of the business.

Bagshaw, John
Lime Street, Newcastle

Mentioned in directories of 1838, 1844, 1850, 1851, 1852, and 1853. In directories of 1855 and 1856 his address is given as 25 Cut Bank, and he is called a china-figure maker.[1] He is not mentioned in a directory of 1857–8, and the site seems to have been taken over by Robert Hall.

Barker, H.
North Shore

This potter is not mentioned in any directory examined, but early directories are rare and several years are missing in the series that were studied.

Jewitt[2] states that a North Shore Pottery was established in Yorkshire near Yarm about 1840 by a Mr James Smith, and continued for many years under several ownerships. None of these seems to have been H. Barker.

A directory of 1821 gives Thomas Fell and Co. as at North Shore, and it appears that from time to time potters occupied a few buildings at St Peter's. H. Barker may have been one of these.

Bell, Isaac   *Phoenix Pottery*
2 Melbourne Street

Mentioned in a directory of 1844. Jewitt[3] says this was the Phoenix Pottery, built by John Dryden & Co.: Isaac Bell was followed by Carr & Patton.

Bell, Isaac, & Galloway and Atkinson   *Albion Pottery*
Ballast Hills, Ouseburn

They succeeded Isaac and Thomas Bell at the Albion Pottery about 1863 but are not recorded in any directory examined. The author has eight Willow pattern plates with their printed mark (m9) and also the impressed mark of their successors, Galloway & Atkinson. Presumably these pieces were made shortly after the take-over of the firm, which appears to have been in 1864.

Bell, Isaac, & Thomas   *Albion Pottery*
Ouseburn

The Bell brothers took over Maling's Ouseburn Bridge Pottery about 1860, and renamed it the Albion Pottery. This followed the dissolution of Bell, Cook & Company at the Phoenix Pottery which the Cook Brothers turned into a

chemical works. About 1863 I. & T. Bell became Isaac **Bell** & Galloway and Atkinson.

Bell, Thomas, & Co.   *Stepney Pottery*
Stepney Bank, Ouseburn

Mentioned in directories of 1847, 1850, 1851, and 1852.

Bell, Cook & Co.   *Phoenix Pottery*
Ouseburn

This firm seems to have taken over the Phoenix Pottery from the Phoenix Pottery Company in 1858–9, and only been in production for a few months. It is not mentioned in directories of these years. When the partnership broke up the Bell brothers took over the Ouseburn Bridge Pottery built by Robert Maling, which they renamed the Albion Pottery, while the Cook brothers converted the Phoenix Pottery into a chemical works in 1860.

Bensham, John Eden

Mentioned in a directory of 1844.

Bird & Co.   *Northumberland Pottery*
Low Lights, North Shields

Mentioned in directories of 1821–2, and 1823. They probably succeeded Collingwood & Beall, and were followed by Cornfoot, Colville & Co.

Blakey, W.   *Railway Bridge Pottery*
Ouseburn

Mentioned in a directory of 1859–60. He succeeded Mr Rogers and was followed in 1860 by Robert Martin & Co.

Blenkinsop, Joseph, & Harl, Ralph *Skinnerburn Pot-house*
Forth Banks

Mentioned by Bourne in his *Newcastle*, 1736, p. 145:
> without the Closegate is a pretty long street with houses on each side; which goes as far as a Dike called Skinnerburn, where are of late years . . . a Pot-house belonging to Mr Joseph Blenkinsop and Ralph Harl . . . .

In 1748 Mr Blenkinsop advertised the factory in the *Journal*, 11 June 1748: '. . . To be lett, situate at the Skinnerburn, the Pot-house now in the possession of Mr Blenkinsop . . .'

Mr Blenkinsop was living in a house without the Closegate in 1749.

In 1758 the pottery was destroyed by fire, it was reported in the *Journal*, 16 September 1758:
> On Wednesday night the Pot-house at the Skinner-burn was burnt down; and but for the timely assistance of the glassmen in all likelihood many of the adjacent buildings would have been consumed.

---

[1] See Introduction, p. 19.
[2] Jewitt, *Ceramic Art of Great Britain*, Vol. II, 1878.
[3] Ibid.

An advertisement in the back of a directory showing the North Shore, c. 1870.

Barker (?). Mug with signature *Barker H. North Shore* beneath the decoration. This may be the signature of the decorator and not the maker of the piece.   (L.A.G.)

Bell, Cook & Co. White and green jug, one of a pair marked M12 and m13.

Bramble. A small jug, copper lustre outside, pink lustre inside. Impressed mark 'S/S Bramble'.

Booth, Taylor
Ouseburn

Mentioned in a directory of 1844.

Bramble   (Location unknown)

While this work was in the press, the author found a copper-lustre jug in a second-hand shop in Newcastle, with the lower two-thirds of the interior of pink-lustre. On the bottom of the jug was a clearly impressed mark 's/s BRAMBLE'. It is most unusual to find copper-lustre marked, and the name Bramble does not seem to have been previously recorded. Until further information becomes available the author believes this piece to have been made on Tyneside ('s/s' may stand for South Shields), but only time and further research will tell.

Brameld & Co.
Folley Wharf, Sandgate

Mentioned in a directory of 1824.

Brougham, John   *Newburn Potwork*
Newburn

John Brougham, a china dealer in Newcastle, established a pot-work at Newburn about 1749. It was a small concern for making garden pottery. The *Journal*, 10 June 1749, reports:

> John Brougham, in the Keyside, Newcastle sells . . . china ware . . . superfine Liverpool and London Delph; also is now made at his Potwork at Newburn, all sorts of Flower Pots for Gardens, ornamental Pots for Summer-houses, Garden Walls or Court Walls, having just pro-cured a professed Workman for that purpose.

Burn, Joseph, & Co.   *Stepney Bank Pottery*
Ouseburn

Mentioned in directories of 1852, 1853, 1855, 1857-8, 1859-60; but is not mentioned in a directory of 1861-2. Joseph Burn succeeded Thomas Bell & Co. at the pottery which had originally been known as the New Pottery, Ouseburn, but was renamed about 1816. He was followed by John Charlton.

Note the close similarity of Burn's Newcastle Arms mark (M15) with that of Fell & Co. This seems to be a deliberate attempt to pass off his wares as those of the leading Tyneside firm of the period.

Burns   *Sheriff Hill Pottery*
Gateshead

Burns carried on the Sheriff Hill Pottery after W. Gray's death in 1906 until he himself died in 1909. The factory appears to have carried on with the same type of business as in the earlier days of the partnership. Burns also owned the Pipewellgate Pottery in Gateshead, but this was only used as a warehouse for the Sheriff Hill Pottery and nothing was produced there. When Burns died he left all his money to the Royal Victoria Infirmary, Newcastle upon Tyne.

Burnside Bros.
5 Lime Street, Ouseburn

Mentioned in directories of 1898, 1899-1900, and 1900. They succeeded J. R. Forster, and when they ceased production, the pottery appears to have closed.

Carr, John   *Low Lights Pottery*
North Shields

Mentioned in directories of 1844, 1847, 1850 when the title is given as Carr (J.) & Co., 1855 with the title Carr, John & Son, 1858, 1874-5 with the title Carr Brothers, 1887-8 as Carr (J.) & Sons and also Carr Bros. & Carr. Apparently there were two businesses at this time; 1889-90, 'Carr (John) & Sons. Potters and fire brick mfrs.'; 1901-2, 'Carr, John & Sons Firebrick manufacturers 44 Low Lights'; 1907-8 'John Carr & Sons Firebrick manufacturers'. This seems to be the last directory entry of the firm, and the pottery side seems to have been abandoned between 1890 and 1901, after which the firm concentrated on the production of firebricks.

The Low Lights pottery appears to have been erected in 1814, possibly for Collingwood and Beall. John Carr and John Patton were in partnership around 1844, Carr eventually taking over the business at North Shields, and John Patton the Phoenix Pottery, Ouseburn.

Carr, John, and Sons

John Carr & Sons manufactured earthenware for the home market and the Mediterranean trade. They ground flint by the Alsung or dry process, and manufactured terracotta vases and articles for the building trade.

The stag's head mark (M25) is said to be very rare, but this may be due to a high proportion of poor impressions. Two pieces in the author's collection could only be recognised by comparison with a well marked piece, and by an accompanying printed mark respectively.

Carr & Patton   *Phoenix Pottery*
Ouseburn

Mentioned in a directory of 1847 as earthenware manu-facturers, Phoenix Pottery, Ouseburn, and North Shields. The partnership seems to have been dissolved about 1848, John Carr continuing at the Low Lights Pottery, North Shields; and John Patton at the Phoenix Pottery, Ouseburn. The latter passed into the hands of the Phoenix Pottery Company about 1856.

J. Burn. Willow pattern side plate, marked M14 and m15, thus identifying the latter, which occurs frequently alone.

J. Burn. Wild Rose pattern side plate (compare with Fells' much better piece, p. 117).

J. Carr & Co. Tonquin pattern plate, marked M16 and m20. (M.B.)

J. Carr & Sons. Asiatic pheasant side plate marked with M23 and m24.

J. Carr & Sons. Pink lustre-ware tureen marked with M25.

J. Carr & Sons. Blue and white geometric design shallow bowl, marked M25 and m26.

Charlton, John   *Ouseburn Bridge Pottery*
Ouseburn

Mentioned in a directory of 1841 with 'brown' against his name. Apparently he seems to have made brown-ware, probably exclusively.

A directory of 1844 gives his address as at the Railway Bridge Pottery, Ouseburn, and Lawson Street. Directories of 1850, 1852, 1853 give his address as Ouseburn. There is then a gap of nine years before the name John Charlton again appears in the directories; either he went out of business and then came back, or perhaps the John Charlton in the directory of 1861–2 is a different individual. The address is given as Ouseburn. A directory of 1863–4 gives the address as Crawford Row, while those of 1865–6 1867–8, 1869–70, 1870–71, 1871–2, 1873–4, and 1874–5 give the address as Crawford's Row, or Ouseburn. He is not mentioned in a directory after 1875.

Charlton, Ralph   *Ouseburn Flint Mill*

Mentioned in directories of 1837 and 1838.

Chatto, William, & Griffiths   *St Anthony's Pottery*
St Anthony's, Newcastle

The pottery at St Anthony's and a leasehold mill at Newburn were taken over from King & Co. in 1787; as reported in the *Courant* for 28 April 1787:

St Anthon's [*sic*] Pottery.

Chatto and Griffith are now carrying on this manufactory in all its Branches to the greatest extent; and they have a large assortment of Queen's or Cream-coloured Earthen Ware, and also of Common Black and Brown Ware, ready for sale upon the lowest terms. N.B. Orders of Exportation will be particularly attended to.

William Chatto became bankrupt about 1795, and William Huntley obtained control. The *Advertiser*, 9 May 1795, carried a notice:

To be sold or let and entered upon immediately, all that commodious and extensive Pottery situated at St. Anthon's [*sic*], near Newcastle, dwelling houses, etc. The premises are well adapted for the exportation and coast trade, which is now well established, and the Manufacture will be carried on till disposed of.

The *Chronicle*, 30 May 1795, mentioned the bankruptcy of 'William Chatto of St Anthon's' [*sic*].

Codling, John   *Heworth Shore Pottery*
Heworth Shore

Mentioned in a directory of 1828 as an earthenware manufacturer. This pottery may have been in the site of that of Thomas Sill.[4]

Codling, Thomas   *Heworth Shore Pottery*

By 1833 the firm was known as Codling & Co. In the same

year a directory gives Patterson, Dawson & Codling, Heworth Shore, Gateshead. Thomas Codling may have succeeded John Codling.

Collingwood & Beall
North Shields

This firm has not been found in any of the directories available, though there are gaps in the earlier numbers. The mark illustrated (m29) occurs on a pink lustre jug beneath a sentimental verse.[5]

Cooper, J.
25 Cut Bank, Ouseburn

Mentioned in directories of 1859–60 and 1861–2. A directory of 1863–4 mentions 'Cooper, T. 25 Cut Bank'. The 'T' is probably an error for 'J'.

Cornfoot, Carr & Patton   *North Shields Pottery*
Low Lights

Mentioned in a directory of 1834. They succeeded Cornfoot, Patton & Co., and were followed by Carr & Patton.

Cornfoot, Colville & Co.   *Low Lights Pottery*
North Shields

They succeeded Mr Nicholas Bird in about 1829, and were followed by Cornfoot, Patton & Co.

Cornfoot, Patton & Co.   *Low Lights Pottery*
North Shields

They succeeded Messrs. Cornfoot, Colville & Co. and were followed by Cornfoot, Carr & Patton.

Cullen, F. J.   *China-ware Dealer*
Newcastle

A plate in the author's possession is back-stamped with this dealer's name.[6]

Cullen & Sons   *China-ware Dealers*
41 Pilgrim Street, Newcastle

They were mentioned in a directory of 1903–4, and as some of the earthenware they sold was back-marked with their name they may be mistaken for manufacturers.

[4] See p. 104.

[5] See p. 18.
[6] See also Cullen & Sons below.

Dale & Head
Ouseburn   *New Pottery*

Mentioned in a directory of 1790, and described as being below Stepney Hill. The pottery was founded about 1786 probably by Dale and Head who were certainly the proprietors in 1790. The following year John Head advertised in the *Advertiser*, 28 May 1791, for a partner: 'A Partner wanted in an established Pottery in the neighbourhood of Newcastle, who will take an active part. Enquire of Mr John Head, Newcastle.'

This almost certainly refers to the New Pottery. John Dalton accepted the partnership, and a Newcastle directory of 1801 records Head and Dalton as proprietors.

Dalton, Burn & Co.   *Stepney Pottery*
Stepney Street, Ouseburn

Mentioned in directories of 1833, 1837, 1838, 1841, and in 1844 as Dalton & Burn.

They succeeded Davies, Cookson & Wilson, and were followed by John Harrison, who appears to have taken possession in 1844.

Dalton, John, & Son   *New Pottery*
Ouseburn

Mentioned in a directory of 1811. The firm succeeded Head & Dalton, and were followed by Dryden, Coxon & Basket. While in the possession of Dalton & Son the pottery was renamed the Stepney Bank Pottery.

Davies, Richard, & Co.   *Tyne Main Pottery*
Salt Meadows, South Shore, Gateshead

Mentioned in directories of 1833, 1837, and 1838. The pottery appears to have been built in 1831 by Richard Davies & Co. and sold to R. C. Wilson in 1844. Davies & Co. produced white-, printed-, and lustre-ware, chiefly for the Norwegian market. They also produced 'Gaudy Welsh'.

Davies, Cookson & Wilson   *Stepney Pottery*
Ouseburn

Mentioned in directories of 1824, 1827, 1828–9, 1829. They succeeded John Dryden & Co., and were followed by Dalton, Burn & Co.

Dawson, Jacob
Heworth Shore

Mentioned in a directory of 1828 as being an earthenware manufacturer. By 1833 he seems to have been in the partnership of Patterson, Dawson & Codling.

Dryden, John, & Co.   *Stepney Pottery*
Ouseburn   and later at the *Phoenix Pottery*

Mentioned in directories of 1821–2, and 1823 as being at the Stepney Pottery; then the firm seems to have been for a short time at St Peter's Pottery while new premises, the Phoenix Pottery, were being built. The Phoenix Pottery opened in 1827, and this address is given in directories of 1827, 1828–9, 1833, 1838, and 1844. They produced filters in addition to blue and white earthenware. In 1844 the factory passed to Isaac Bell.

Dryden, Coxon & Basket   *Stepney Bank Pottery*
Ouseburn

This firm followed John Dalton & Son about 1816, and by 1821 the factory had passed into the control of John Dryden & Co.

Durham China Company
Earlsway, Team Valley Trading Estate, County Durham

After World War II the socialist government decided to set up a continental china factory on the Team Valley Estate. In 1950 a pilot scheme began in a few Nissen huts, and with a grant of £250,000 from the government a large new factory was built in little over a year. The managing director was a Czechoslovakian refugee whose family had owned a china works in Karlspart; several other senior men were from the continent, and production of feldspar china to Czechoslovakian formulae began in June 1951.

The new firm encountered difficulties in recruiting skilled labour, and had trouble in glazing and firing; the lips of many of the cups and mugs were rough and unpleasant to use. They concentrated on dinner services, coffee sets, and Coronation mugs and plates, decorated with lithographic overglaze transfers probably imported from Germany. They also sold considerable quantities of plain china to small firms who decorated and refired it.

Though the feldspar china was greyish in colour, it was considerably cheaper than the traditional white bone-china of Staffordshire, and the Midland firms feared this competition. Pressure appears to have been placed on the suppliers of the raw materials, and credit facilities granted to the new firm were very stringent. The company ran into financial difficulties, and by Christmas 1953 was in the hands of a receiver, who tried to rescue the venture. Dr Worm, a German ceramic expert, was consulted on reorganisation; but the company's finances did not improve, and its assets were put up to auction in July 1954, thus ending the only attempt at china production, as distinct from earthenware, on Tyneside. The glost kiln was purchased by Adamsez of Scotswood, and is still in use. Some of the plate machines were bought by the Royal Art Pottery at Stoke.

Politics and emotion obscure the facts behind this failure. Strong local feelings were aroused by the ill-starred venture: on the one hand big business was held to have strangled a dangerous rival; on the other a political project was considered to have devoured a quarter of a million pounds of public money in producing an inferior product, while long established firms were refused aid in recovering from the

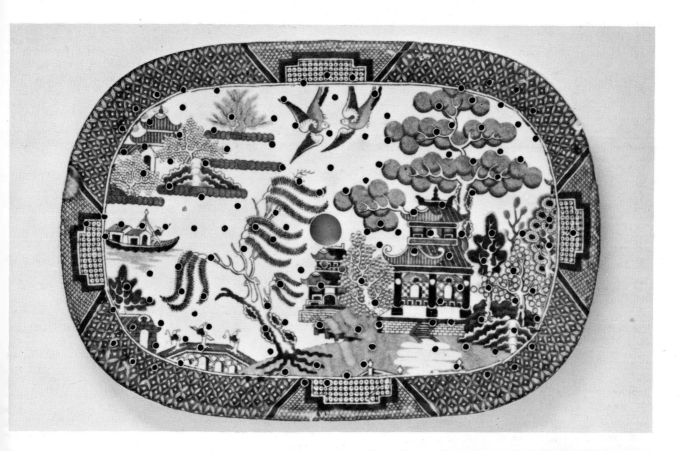

R. Davies & Co. Willow pattern fish strainer, marked M30.

R. Davies & Co. Small plate in 'Gaudy Welsh' style, marked M30.

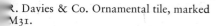

R. Davies & Co. Ornamental tile, marked M31.

ULYSSES FOLLOWING THE CAR OF NAUSICAA
WITH SKILL THE VIRGIN GUIDES TH' EMBROIDER'D REIN
SLOW ROLLS THE CAR BEFORE TH' ATTENDING TRAIN.

View of the Durham China Company's factory and chimney, in 1951. (Courtesy of the Dunlop Rubber Co.)

Sketch of the layout of the Durham China Pottery as remembered by one of the former workmen.

Chimney	Engineering	Biscuit kiln (1375° to 1700°C)	Glost kiln (900°C)	Design centre		
Mills		Glazing room (women)			Decorating (mostly overglaze)	Muffle kiln
Mills		Driers		Moulds		
		Plate and cup making				

Durham China Company. Feldspathic porcelain plate with overglaze decoration, marked m32.

stresses of the war. Perhaps the truth lies somewhere between these two views.

The sketch on p. 56 shows the layout of the factory as remembered by one of the Czechoslovakian workmen who is still employed in the same building by the Dunlop Rubber Company. He relates the following story: When the chimney was nearly finished some of his friends dared him to climb it. He set off up the ladder inside the chimney, becoming increasingly nervous as he neared the top. On arrival he was horrified to see the ground so far below; a horror increased by discovering that the mortar between the last few feet of bricks was still soft. Memories of this moment give him palpitations!

Eden, John
Bensham, Gateshead

Mentioned in a directory of 1844.

Elliot, H., & Co.   *Ouseburn Pottery*
Ouseburn

Mentioned in directories of 1821–2 and 1823. He seems to have succeeded Robert Yellowley and been followed by James Tuer and Co.

Fell, Isaac, & Co   *Carr's Hill Pottery*
Gateshead   Later at *Tyne* or *South Shields Pottery*

A directory of 1847 mentions Isaac and Joseph Fell, earthenware manufacturers, as living at St Lawrence; but does not give their place of business. Directories of 1867–8, and 1870–1 give 'Fell (I) & Co. Carr's Hill'; and in 1871 Isaac Fell and George S. Young bought the Tyne or South Shields Pottery and continued manufacture there for several years.

G. B. Hodgson[7] wrote:

The Tyne or South Shields Pottery was established in Waterloo Vale about 1830, by a Mr Robertson, from whom, about eleven years later, it passed into the hands of Mr John Armstrong. He continued the works for thirty years, enlarging them during that period. In 1871 they were purchased by Messrs. Isaac Fell and George S. Young, who continued the trade for several years under the style of Messrs. Isaac Fell & Co. The class of goods manufactured were 'Sunderland' and 'brown' wares, of which large quantities were shipped to the Continent and supplied to London and the home markets. The earthenware was manufactured from the common brick clay of the neighbourhood, and after drying was lined inside with white slip, and glazed with lead and glaze. The *Tyne Pottery* was in its day the largest in the district, except for the works of Messrs. Harwood of Stockton, for this kind of pottery. It has, however, been closed and dismantled for some years [1903].

Fell, Thomas, & Co.   *St Peter's Pottery*
St Peter's,[8] Newcastle

The pottery was built by Thomas Bell and Thomas Fell in 1817; trading as Thomas Fell & Co. A directory of 1821 gives Fell, Thomas & Co., North Shore.[9] A directory of 1824 gives the address as St Peter's Quay. The company is listed in directories of 1821–2, 1823, 1824, 1827, 1827–8, 1829, 1833, 1838, 1844, 1847, 1850, 1852, 1853, 1855, 1857–8, 1858, 1859–60, 1861–2, 1863–4, 1865–6, 1867–8, 1869–70, 1870–1, 1871–2. In the directory of 1873–4 the company is listed as 'Fell T. & Co. (Limited)' for the first time and then in 1874–5, 1877, 1877–8, 1879, 1880, 1881–2, 1883, 1883–4, 1884, 1885–6, 1887, 1887–8, 1888, 1889–90, 1890, but the firm is not recorded in the directory of 1891–2. Kelly's directory of Northumberland of 1894 lists 'Fell & Co. St Peter's', but this is probably a mistake, and the entry retained through an oversight.[10]

Fell & Co. manufactured all kinds of white, sponged, printed and enamelled goods for home and export markets. In 1869 Fell & Co. became a limited liability company under the same title, the shareholders being descendants of the original proprietors. The firm mainly produced white and coloured domestic earthenware, the amount of lustreware being small. Under the limited liability company only printed pieces were marked, and these usually bear the full name, 'Fell & Co.', though the abbreviation T F & Co. was also used.

Richardson[11] refers to the St Peter's Pottery:

Aug. 13, 1837. Sunday, between the hours of one and two in the afternoon, a fire was discovered in Messrs. Fell & Co.'s pottery, at St Peter's, near Newcastle.

In a short time three engines were on the ground. The fire by this time had made great progress, but was gradually got under. It was not extinguished till between four and five o'clock. The damage was estimated at between £500 and £600. The property was insured in the North British Fire Office. The fire was supposed to have originated in one of the stores.

T. Fell & Co. exhibited at the 1862 Exhibition in London; the relevant entry in the official catalogue reads:

No. 6852 Class 35

Fell T. & Co. Dinner ware, vase, table top, lamps, chamberware.

(They do not appear to have been awarded any medal or prize for their exhibits.)

The marks are difficult to date but the earliest pieces made between 1817 and 1830 are impressed with M33 or 'FELL'. Later the mark M37 was used; and in about 1840 the Newcastle Arms with 'FELL' or 'F & Co' beneath. When the firm became a limited company in 1869 the mark seems to have been changed to 'T F & Co'.

---

[8] St Peter's is a corruption of St Peter's Quay, a wharf leased from the Corporation of Newcastle by Sir Peter Riddell. The lease is dated '20 March 5 Car. 1' (A.D. 1630).

[9] See also H. Barker, p. 46.

[10] See p. 147.

[11] M. A. Richardson, *The Local Historian's Table Book of Remarkable Occurrences, Historical Facts, Traditional Legendary and Descriptive Ballads etc. etc. connected with the Counties of Newcastle upon Tyne, Northumberland and Durham*, London, 1840, Volume 4, p. 375.

[7] G. B. Hodgson, *Borough of South Shields*, Newcastle upon Tyne, 1903, p. 408.

Fell & Co. Large blue and white geometric design cheese plate, 16 inch diameter, marked M37.

Fell & Co. Moulded green plate with vine leaf design, marked M37.

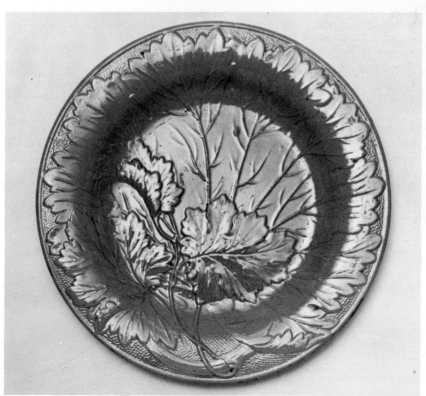

Fell & Co. Bowl with gilded rim. Dated June 28th, 1829, and marked with M36.

Left.
Fell & Co. Polychrome pot-pourri jar marked with M35 on the side of the base. (L.A.G.)

Fell & Co. Basket decorated with Bosphorous design and marked M37 and m46. (L.A.G.)

Fell & Co. Two blue and white **salad** plates with different rural scenes, marked M37.

Fell & Co. Classical scene in light blue on a large side plate, marked M37.

Fell & Co. Dark blue Willow pattern side plate marked M37 and m42.

Fell & Co. Light blue Willow pattern side plate marked M37 and a mark similar to m50 but with WILLOW printed above the crown.

Fell & Co. Jug, probably commemorating
the 300th anniversary of the death of
Shakespeare, marked m52.

Fenwick, C. W.
7 Lime Street, Ouseburn

Mentioned in directories of 1865–6 and 1867–8. The first of these contains an advertisement which reads: 'C. W. Fenwick, Yellow Baker, and Black & Rockingham, Teapot manufacturer, Lime Street, Newcastle-on-Tyne.'

Ferry, John
Sheriff Hill, Gateshead

Mentioned in a directory of 1837.

Fordy, J., & Co.   *Sheriff Hill Pottery*
Gateshead

Mentioned in a directory of 1824. He seems to have succeeded Jackson & Co., and been followed by Fordy and Patterson.

Fordy, Patterson & Co.   *Sheriff Hill Pottery*
Gateshead

Mentioned in directories of 1827, 1827–8, and 1829. They appear to have succeeded J. Fordy & Co. about 1826, and to have been followed by Jackson & Patterson about 1833.

Forster, J.
25 Cut Bank, Ouseburn

A directory of 1861–2 mentions 'J. Forster of 119 Piperwellgate, Gateshead', and the following directory of 1863–4 gives 'J. Forster, 25 Cut Bank'. These entries would seem to refer to the same individual. He apparently succeeded J. Cooper.

Forster, John Rennie
7 Lime Street, Ouseburn

Mentioned in directories of 1888, 1889–90, 1890, 1891–2, 1892, 1893–4, 1894, 1895–6, 1897–8. The directories of 1893–4, 1895–6 and 1897–8 give his address as 5 Lime Street. He may have moved to a different pottery alongside his first one.
In 1898, 5 Lime Street was occupied by Burnside Brothers.

Foster & Cutter   *St Anthony's Pottery*
St Anthony's

A directory of 1801 gives 'Forsyth & Cutter, potters, St Anthony's'. This seems to be an error for Foster. Foster and Cutter obtained the pottery from William Huntley in 1800, and were followed by Mr Joseph Sewell in 1804.

Galloway & Atkinson   *Albion Pottery*
Ballast Hills, Ouseburn

They succeeded Isaac Bell, Galloway & Atkinson about

1864, and were followed by William Atkinson who is first mentioned in a directory of 1865–6. The author obtained fourteen Willow pattern plates, six of which bore the impressed mark of the firm (M54) and eight the impressed mark with the addition of the printed mark of Isaac Bell & Galloway and Atkinson (m9). These plates seem to have been made immediately after the take-over, and are probably a little older than the six first mentioned.

Gardener, J.
7 Lime Street, Ouseburn

Mentioned in a directory of 1870–1. A directory of 1871–2 spells his name differently, and gives a different number to the address: 'Gardner, J., 6 Lime Street.'
He seems to have succeeded T. R. Leighton, and was followed by Mould & Stonehouse.

Gateshead Art Pottery Company
East Street

Mentioned in a directory of 1884.

Gibson, J.
St Anthony's

Mentioned in a directory of 1858. This seems to have been a small brown-ware pottery.

Gray, George   *Railway Bridge Pottery*
Ouseburn

A directory of 1847 lists George Gray as an earthenware manufacturer with a business in Ouseburn, and living at Byker Buildings. He is also mentioned in directories of 1850 and 1851 and was succeeded by Mr Rogers.

Grey, G., & Co.   *Jarrow Brown-ware Pottery*
Gateshead

Mentioned in a directory of 1851.

Gray & Burns   *Sheriff Hill Pottery*
Gateshead

This firm was formed after the death of Robinson about 1902, and continued until Gray's death in 1906. About this time some of the workers came from Thornaby-on-Tees and strengthened the labour force. After his partner's death Burns carried on alone.
The firm made pottery hardware jars for Forster Blackett of Gallowgate Lead Works, and also dishes, mugs, etc., which were sold on Tyneside, especially in Blaydon and Ryton.

Hall, Robert
25 Cut Bank, Ouseburn

Mentioned in a directory for 1857–8. At the back was an advertisement: 'Robert Hall. Manufacturer of Black & Rockingham Teapots and Yellow Bakers. No. 25 Cut Bank, Ouseburn, Newcastle-upon-Tyne.'

Hardy, Thomas   *Carr's Hill Pottery*
Gateshead

Mentioned in directories of 1877–8, 1879, 1878–80, 1881–2. He appears to have succeeded Lowry & Hardy, and been followed by J. Hopper.

Harrison, John   *Stepney Bank Pottery*
Ouseburn

Mentioned in a directory of 1844 as being at the Ouseburn Pottery. He seems to have succeeded Dalton & Burn, and been followed by Thomas Bell & Co.

Head & Dalton   *New Pottery*
Ouseburn

Mentioned in a directory of 1801. Dalton joined Head in partnership in 1791, the new firm succeeding that of Dale & Head. They were followed by John Dalton & Son, who renamed the factory The Stepney Bank Pottery.

Hebburn Quay Pottery

There is a reference to this factory in the *Journal*, 9 July and 18 November 1757: 'To be let a good and convenient Pot-house at Hebburn Key [sic], for the making of Earthen and Stone ware.'

Note this early reference to 'Stone ware', though pieces did not carry this description until after 1840.

Hepworth, John
62 Close

Mentioned in a directory of 1883

Heworth Common Pottery
Gateshead

This pottery was active in 1759 and 1760 making tortoise-shell-, agatestone- and black-ware. It was possibly owned by Robert Callendar of Newcastle. Two references appeared in local papers; in the *Journal*, 3 November 1757:

Wanted immediately, and will be let upon reasonable terms, a Copartnership in a current-going Pottery on Heworth Common, near Gateshead Turnpike Bar, commodiously situated for Clay and Coals. Where is made Tortoishell [sic], Agatestone and Black Ware to great perfection, with a Variety of other kinds of Earthen Ware.

In the *Courant*, 10 May 1760:

To be let or sold, a Potwork situate on Heworth Common, near Gateshead Turnpike Bar, where is made to great perfection Tortoishell [sic], Agatestone and Black Ware, with a variety of other kinds of Earthen Ware. Likewise a Flint Mill, Stamp Mill and Layth, and all other Utensils. There is also a compleat set of Moulds of the newest and best patterns. Enquire of Mr Robert Callendar of Newcastle. The principal workman attends the Work and will show the premises.

Hillcoat, William   *South Shore Pot-house*
Gateshead

This business was operative at least as early as 1757 when the following appeared in the *Journal*, 12 February:

Whereas Joseph Warburton has been employed for some years in making China at Bow near London. He does hereby make known to the publick that he finds better materials here for the purpose, and to be had at a cheaper rate. Therefore any gentleman willing to encourage such an undertaking may know particulars of the expense by applying to the above Joseph Warburton at Mr Hilcot's [sic] Pot-house on the South Shore.

In the *Journal*, 4 March 1769, the following advertisement appeared:

William Hillcoat is just returned from the South where he has purchased from the best Manufacturers a large assortment of Cream colour'd and white Stone Plates and Dishes, which he proposes selling on the Quay by retail at the wholesale prices, viz. superfine white stone Table Plates at 2s. per Dozen; and every other article in proportion; also a large assortment of oriental china figures. He likewise manufactures Cream colour'd and all other sorts of Earthen Ware.

William Hillcoat was both a manufacturer and a dealer in earthenware.

An open market is still held on the quayside at Newcastle on Sunday mornings, when china, earthenware, cloth, tinned goods and other items are offered for sale.

Hillcoat, Brown & Backhouse   *Ouseburn Pottery*
Ouseburn

Mentioned in a directory of 1790. They succeeded Backhouse, Hillcoat & Co. Brown had a half share in the business and was the principal manager of the pottery. The firm produced all kinds of fine pottery, including cream-ware. They were followed by Robert Yellowley. There are two newspaper references to the firm, one in the *Chronicle*, 13 November 1790: 'Thomas Stoddart, an apprentice to Messrs. Hillcoat and Company of the Ouseburn Pottery, as a painter did absent himself from his said Masters.'

Another in the *Chronicle*, 20 November 1790: 'T. Stoddart replies to the above. His indenture and bond were voluntarily given up to him by Mr Brown, who was half owner and Principal Manager of the Pottery Concern.'

Hillevat, A.
Ouseburn

Mentioned in a directory of 1850, but not in one of the following year.

Hodgson, J. B.   *Jarrow Pottery*
Gateshead

Mentioned in directories of 1852 and 1853. He succeeded G. Grey & Co. who produced brown-ware, and the new firm probably carried on the same type of work. The pottery appears to have closed before the 1855 directory was published.

Hollingshead, James   *Ouseburn Pottery*
Ouseburn

It is not clear if this is the same Ouseburn Pottery occupied by John Maling between 1837 and 1864; and whether the two firms used the same building, or if there were two separate potteries of the same name.

James Hollingshead is mentioned in directories of 1850, 1851, 1852, 1853, 1855, 1857-8, 1858, 1859-60, but is omitted from the directory of 1861-2. In three of the directories he is listed as a figure-maker,[12] and in the 1855 directory is given two addresses: Ouseburn and Quay.

Holmes, John
Stepney Square, Ouseburn

Mentioned in directories of 1850, 1851, 1852, 1853, 1855, 1857-8, 1858; but not thereafter.

Hopper, J.   *Carr's Hill Pottery*
Gateshead

Mentioned in a directory of 1883-4. He appears to have succeeded T. Hardy, and been followed by Thomas Patterson.

Humble & Morris
St Lawrence, Newcastle

Mentioned in a directory of 1855. At the end of the directory is an advertisement: 'J. Humble & Co. St. Lawrence. Sanitary works & Pottery. Water closets, plug bowls, ornamental stands, ware pipes for sewerage, etc. Warehouse 17 Union Street and 26 Groat Market, N'cle on Tyne.' He was also a dealer in earthenware, glass, etc.

Huntley, William   *St Anthony's Pottery*
St Anthony's

William Huntley took over control of the pottery from Chatto and Griffiths in 1795, but in 1800 he was succeeded by Foster and Cutter.

[12] See Introduction, p. 19.

The following announcement appeared in the *Chronicle*, 29 March 1800:

To be sold by private contract, the Pottery at St Anthon's [*sic*], lately occupied by Mr William Huntley, and held by lease from the late Thomas Lewins, Esq. 22 years of which will be unexpired at Lammas next. Apply to Mr Chatto, Westgate Street, Newcastle.

Hutchinson, Edward
15 Lime Street, Ouseburn

Mentioned in directories of 1877-8, 1879, 1878-80, 1881-2, 1883, 1883-4, 1885-6. The directory of 1883 gives his address as '7 Lime Street', and the last two directories as '5 Lime Street'. He may have changed his premises, or there may have been a renumbering of the street.

Jackson, Paul   *Sheriff Hill Pottery*
Gateshead

Mentioned in a directory of 1778. The pottery had been established at least five years earlier as can be seen from the *Journal*, 25 December 1773: 'Earthen Ware sold by Mr Paul Jackson at his shop on the quay, Newcastle . . . and at his Factory on Gateshead Common near the Common Alehouse adjoining Durham Road.'

Another advertisement in the *Chronicle*, 12 August 1775, tells us:

P. Jackson, Pilgrim Street, Newcastle, having brought his different kinds of Earthen Ware to great perfection, hopes for Encouragement from his Friends. He sells wholesale and retail at his Manufactory on Gateshead Common, adjoining the Turnpike Road and near the Two-mile Stone, and at his shop on the Quay, Cream-coloured, enamelled, fine black, gilded, spotted and brown Earthen Ware; also large Ware, as Milk, Cream, Butter and Beef Pots and Washing Mugs. Hawkers from Northumberland and Cumberland may be supplied at his shop.

Paul Jackson died in 1787, and his sons William and Collingwood Forster Jackson succeeded to the business.

Jackson, William, & Collingwood Forster   *Sheriff Hill*
Gateshead   *Pottery*

W. & C. F. Jackson succeeded to their father's business on the latter's death in 1787. Two notices in a local paper of 1788 are of interest. In the *Courant*, 22 November 1788: 'Apprentices absconded. Isabella Hall and Clifford Grieve, painters of Earthen Ware, Apprentices at Sheriff-hill Pottery, in the parish of Gateshead, have absented themselves from the manufactory.' In the *Courant*, 29 November 1788: 'The Warehouse of Sheriff Hill Pottery was broken into (. . . and money taken) Reward of Five Guineas offered by Messrs. W. and C. F. Jackson, Proprietors of the said pottery.'

W. & C. F. Jackson are in a list of merchants published in the *Chronicle*, 25 February 1797, who agreed to accept local bank-notes.

William Jackson died in 1798, and C. F. Jackson is

described in 1801 as carrying on the business. The latter probably sold it before 1811.

Directories of 1787 and 1790 list 'William & C. F. Jackson, Pilgrim Street'. This would have been their retail establishment.

Jackson & Co   *Sheriff Hill Pottery*
Gateshead Fell

Mentioned in a directory of 1801. After the death of William Jackson in 1798, his brother C. F. Jackson may have taken on a partner. From the entry in the directory the company would appear to have changed its name. It probably ceased before 1811.

Jackson & Patterson   *Sheriff Hill Pottery*
Gateshead

Mentioned in directories of 1833, 1837, 1838. The directories of 1833 and 1838 also give an address of '37 Quay side'. This would have been a retail establishment. Jackson and Patterson succeeded Fordy & Patterson, and were followed by John Ferry.

Kendall, Matthew   *Carr's Hill Pottery*
Gateshead

Mentioned in directories of 1851, 1853, and 1855. He followed Kendall & Walker, and was succeeded by Isaac Fell & Co. after an interval of several years.

Kendall, Matthew, & Walker, John   *Carr's Hill Pottery*
Gateshead

Mentioned in a directory of 1844 as earthenware manufacturers. By 1852 the firm had become M. Kendall.

King, James, & Co.   *St Anthony's Pottery*
Newcastle

The Local Historian's Table Book,[13] contains an extract from local papers:

> May 16, 1784. A fire broke out in the pottery of St Anthony's, on the river Tyne, near Newcastle, belonging to Messrs. King and Co., but was got under after damaging a great quantity of earthenware and part of the building.

James King & Co. also had interests in several glass works. A series of misfortunes overtook the pottery side of the firm, and in 1786 James King became bankrupt, forcing a sale of the pottery. An advertisement gives an insight into the industry at this period: from the *Courant*, 1 July 1786:

> Pottery to be sold. The leasehold premises situated at St Anthon's [*sic*] near Newcastle, lately used by James King & Co. for carrying on a Pottery Manufactory. The premises will be sold in the following lots:

> Lot I.   That part of the premises used in manufacturing Cream-coloured, Blue and White, and Enamelled Wares.
> Lot II.   That part of the premises used in manufacturing Black and Brown Wares.
> Lot III.   A leasehold Mill at Newburn, for grinding Flints and other pottery materials.

The property was taken over by Chatto and Griffiths in 1787.

King, Marshall   *Low Lights Pottery*
North Shields

King took over the Low Lights Pottery from John Carr & Sons about 1890, and used the premises as a wholesale warehouse. He had his wares back-stamped with 'M. KING & CO. THE POTTERY NORTH SHIELDS' and the author has pieces with this mark associated with those of Bishop & Stonier of Hanley, Staffordshire, and C. T. Maling, Newcastle.

In 1892–5 King took over the Sheriff Hill Pottery, but failed to make it pay, and sold it to Robinson, Gray & Burns. At this time he seems to have been a manufacturer as well as a wholesale merchant.

In directories of 1901–2, 1903–4, and 1905–6 his address is given as 10 Pape Buildings, Pink Lane, Newcastle. This would have been his head office. In the 1911–12 directory the address is given as Cross Street, Newcastle.

M. King & Co., wholesale pottery suppliers and merchants, are still in business in Upper Queen Street, North Shields.

Kirton, J., & Co.
Ouseburn

Mentioned in a directory of 1861–2.

Kirton & Leathead
Ouseburn

Mentioned in a directory of 1859–60.

Laing, W.
Lime Street, Ouseburn

Mentioned in a directory of 1877.

Lee, John   *Acomb Pottery*
near Hexham, Northumberland

Nothing is known of the Acomb pottery, apart from the following newspaper advertisement from the *Journal*, 10 November 1764:

> To be sold, a pottery at or near a village called Acomb, within 1½ miles of Hexham, lately belonging to Mr. Lee of Acomb, but now belonging to Mr John Lee his son. A very convenient and well fitted up pottery for all sorts of Brown Black and Tortoise-shell Ware.

[13] Richardson, op. cit., Vol. II, p. 295.

Lees, Aaron
Old Customs House Quay, North Shields

Mentioned in a directory of 1827.

Leighton, T. R.
7 Lime Street, Ouseburn

Mentioned in a directory of 1869–70. He seems to have succeeded C. W. Fenwick, and been followed by J. Gardener.

Lewins & Parsons   *Sheriff Hill Pottery*
Gateshead

According to Jewitt,[14] Messrs. Lewins and Parsons had a pottery at Sheriff Hill for the manufacture of the commoner kinds of earthenware. Their firm has not been found in available directories.

Lloyd, William   *St Anthony's Pottery*
St Anthony's

The St Anthony's pottery was closed by Sewell & Co. in 1878, but was re-opened in 1882 by Mr Lloyd. His name appears in directories of 1883, and 1883–4. The firm then became Lloyd & Hodges.

Lloyd & Hodges   *St Anthony's Pottery*
St Anthony's

Mentioned in a directory of 1885–6. Mr William Lloyd seems to have taken a junior partner, but the firm only lasted a year or so. They were followed in 1891–2 by Patterson & Parkinson.

Lowry & Hardy   *Carr's Hill Pottery*
Gateshead

Mentioned in directories of 1873–4, and 1874–5. They succeeded Isaac Fell & Co., and in 1877 Thomas Hardy carried on the business alone.

Maling, Christopher Thompson *Ouseburn Bridge Pottery*
Ouseburn
later at **Ouseburn** and **Walker**[15] *Ford Potteries (A) & (B)*

Mentioned in directories of 1855, 1857–8, 1858, 1859–60, 1861–2, 1863–4. The directory for 1865–6 gives the address as 'Ford Pottery, Ouseburn' and this continues with slight variations in directories of 1867–8, 1869–70, 1870–1, 1871–2, 1873–4, 1874–5, 1877, 1877–8, 1879. A directory of 1878–90 gives the address as 'Ford Street and Walker Road', the latter referring to the New or (B) factory; and this address

continues for directories of 1880, 1881–82, 1883, 1883–4, 1884, 1885–6, 1887, 1887–8, 1889–90, and 1890. The next directory lists the firm as C. T. Maling & Sons.

Christopher Thompson Maling, the second of this name in the family, succeeded his father, Robert Maling, at the Ouseburn Bridge Pottery in 1853. This small factory had only two kilns, and its total production in a year did not equal that of the Ford (A) factory in a week. In 1857 C. T. Maling married Mary, the daughter of John Ford of Edinburgh, of the Holyrood Glassworks. (These closed in 1907.)

In 1859 he built the Ford (A) Pottery, Ouseburn, which occupied about two acres of land, and was a very large pottery in those days. He introduced the newest machinery and processes, and constructed several special machines for his own requirements. By employing machinery whenever possible his wares were more uniform in shape and size than could be produced by hand, and the business expanded rapidly. The Ford (A) Pottery used eighty tons of clay a month to turn out some 750,000 articles. Five government officials were kept fully employed in testing and stamping measuring-jugs and mugs, more than 800,000 tested pieces being passed each year.

C. T. Maling acquired a fortune from the jam pots, jars, bottles for potted meats and dairy products made at the (A) factory, and invested £100,000 building the huge (B) factory half-a-mile away on a 14-acre site in Walker.[16] This was the largest and most complete pottery in Britain. The buildings covered over six and a half acres, and the rest of the area was occupied by mills, workshops, kilns, warehouses, railway lines and sidings, yards, sheds for storing straw, flints, clay and stone. All the processes in manufacture from raw materials to the finished article occurred virtually under one roof. The machinery was driven by steam power. In about 1890, electric lighting was installed in the factory, one of the first in the country to be so equipped; and in the early 1920s steam power was replaced by electricity, over 60 motors from 50 h.p. downwards being in use. The firm had a private railway station, and a packing shed which allowed goods to be stacked in trucks without intermediate cartage.

The flint mill was for many years one of the largest and finest in the country. It was powered by a compound 'Corliss' engine of about 500 h.p. and could grind over 100 tons of flint and Cornwall stone per week. Most of this was used by the firm, but considerable quantities were exported.

Beside these technical advances, C. T. Maling had his own free school at the Ford (A) Pottery before the Education Act of 1870. Among the pupils were Gilroy, the noted commercial artist, and Dr Peters. He also established free soup kitchens.

In 1889 Mr C. T. Maling took his three sons, John Ford Maling, Christopher Thompson Maling jun., and Frederick Theodore Maling into partnership, gradually transferring control of C. T. Maling & Sons to them. He finally retired in 1899, the business continuing under the same name. The Ford (B) factory turned out over 1,500,000 articles per month comprising pots and jars of all shapes and sizes for use by confectioners, marmalade manufacturers, and purveyors of preserved foods. All Keillers marmalade pots were made by Maling. The two factories also produced table ware, and toilet and household utensils.

C. T. Maling died in 1901.

[14] Jewitt, op. cit.
[15] See Appendix I, p. 119.

[16] See p. 93.

C. T. Maling. A photograph of C. T. Maling inserted into a pottery frame, marked similar to m68, but with BRITTANIC PHOTOGRAPH FRAME written along the three sides of the triangle.

C. T. Maling's Ford (A) pottery, built in 1859.

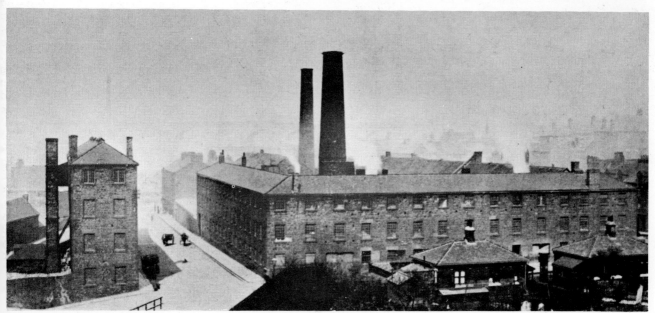

C. T. Maling's Ford (B) pottery built in 1878 on a 14-acre site.

C. T. Maling's Ford (B) pottery from the east.

Advertisement showing the Ford (A) and (B) potteries as they were in 1927.

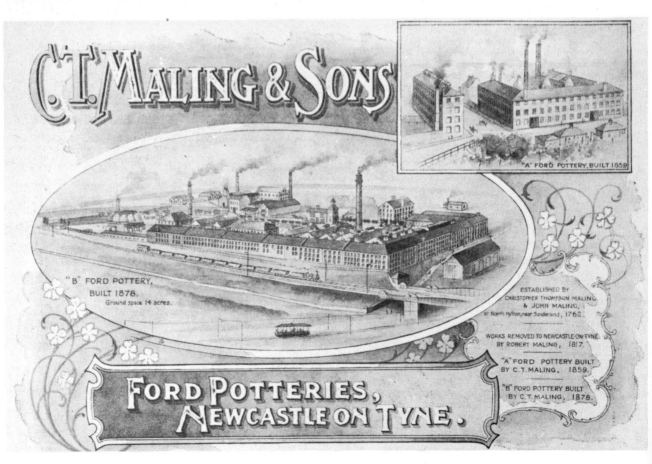

70

C. T. Maling. A small selection of cream
pots made by the Ford factories, marked
m68 or unmarked.   (M.L.S.)

C. T. Maling. A selection of meat-paste
pots made by the Ford factories. Marked
with impressed numbers (pattern numbers)
One has an (A) in addition for (A) factory.
(M.L.S.)

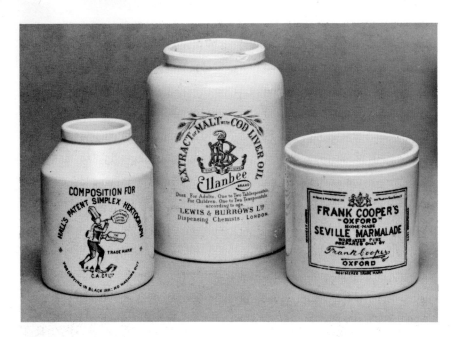

C. T. Maling. Selection of commercial jars. The Oxford Marmalade jar has mark M59, with an additional 'K'. (M.L.S.)

C. T. Maling. A milk crock. (M.L.S.)

C. T. Maling. A cream crock, marked M58. (M.L.S.)

C. T. Maling. Open crock for brewing wine and making bread.   (M.L.S.)

Maling, C. T., & Sons (Ltd) *Ford Potteries* (A) & (B)
Ouseburn and Walker

First mentioned in directories of 1891–2, and then continuously until the closure of the firm in 1963.

Successors to C. T. Maling in 1889, the firm employed 1,000 men and girls in 1901 and were leaders in attending to the well-being of their work-people; the workshops were large and airy and elaborate precautions were taken to lessen dust and improve ventilation. From 1890 onwards *fritted* lead was used, a process by which the lead was converted into glass before being handled, with the virtual elimination of lead poisoning in the factory.

The new firm carried on their predecessor's huge output of commercial jars, including those for Cooper's Oxford Marmalade. Maling pots had been used since the foundation of the firm in 1874 by Mrs Cooper in her kitchen, and continued until the outbreak of World War II in 1939. C. T. Maling & Sons Ltd. also made a variety of table, toilet and household wares, including highly decorated dinner, tea, dessert and bedroom wares, and flower pots. A large staff of artists, designers, engravers, modellers and lithographers was employed, who introduced an impressive series of new shapes and designs, including sanitary ware, hospital utensils, chemists' requisites, dairy containers, cells for electric batteries, and other electrical earthenware, photographic wares and scientific and laboratory equipment.

In the early 1920s the art director of the Ford Potteries was Mr Lucien Boullemier, the son of Anton Boullemier, who came from Sèvres in 1870 to Messrs Mintons. Lucien studied under his father at Mintons before going to Newcastle. Many of the best Maling designs were created by him. He left about 1932 and went to Hanley in Staffordshire.

At the end of World War I, C. T. Maling & Sons had big contracts to supply white-ware to the British government and lustre-ware to firms in Canada and Australia. During the General Strike in 1926 the potters did not refuse to work, but the Ford factories had to close after a few weeks because the coal strike continued for many months, and proper firing of the 'bottle kilns' required the best Throckley or Warbottle coals, which were unobtainable.

During the closure customers went elsewhere; C. T. Maling and Sons never regained their former turnover and (A) pottery was closed. The American slump in the late 'twenties cost Maling their market in the United States; in addition the Staffordshire Potteries dumped their unwanted exports onto the home market and by about 1930 Woolworths began to sell cheap coloured pottery from Hong Kong.[17]

About this time C. T. Maling & Sons received an order for blue and white pottery from the Ringtons Tea Company of Newcastle. These pieces were sold containing one pound of tea, and were marked RINGTONS LIMITED TEA MERCHANTS NEWCASTLE UPON TYNE. Some have an additional small *Maling* beneath; many have no indication of their manufacturer, though all were made at the Ford factory. American collectors are now seeking these pieces, and they are being exported to the United States in considerable numbers.[18]

[17] A selection of dinner services of C. T. Maling, and C. T. Maling & Sons are illustrated on pp. 82–6.
[18] See p. 17.

Ringtons also ordered lustre jugs of various designs and sizes. A fine collection of these pieces is on display at the Rington warehouse, Algernon Road, Heaton. A print of the building itself appears on the bottom of some of these pieces.

The production of cheap glass jars for conserves, and waxed paper cartons and plastic containers for dairy products caused a gradual decline in orders for commercial pottery. In an effort to obtain new custom the firm diversified its products, even at one time making reproduction Sunderland-type lustre-ware for Jacobs, of Berners Street, London.

Impressed marks similar to those illustrated may be found on many Maling pieces manufactured around the turn of the 20th century. 'cc' indicates the use of an ordinary clay body which is light cream in colour; 'ss' refers to the addition of cobalt to whiten the earthenware (sometimes called semi-porcelain) to look more like porcelain.

The numbers are dates, 1199 being November 1899, 890 being August 1890, 998 being September 1898, 401 being April 1901.

During World War II the production of coloured ware was prohibited by the government as an economy measure, and C. T. Maling & Sons were left with considerable supplies of decorated pottery which could not be sold. More disastrous was the loss of skilled craftsmanship through lack of practice and training. In 1947 the pottery was acquired by Hoults Estates Ltd, controllers of the well-known furniture removal contractors, Hoults Removals, Ltd. The directors were Mr Frederick Hoult and Mr Edward Hoult.

Maling, C. T., & Sons (Hoults Ltd.)

Mr Frederick Hoult was very interested in his new acquisition, and encouraged the potters to experiment with novel designs. Unfortunately the loss of skill during the war years, and the retirement of many employees with the change of management, affected the quality of the pottery. The wares of this last period were heavier, and the decoration more garish, than those produced by the Maling family.

C. T. Maling & Sons under Mr Frederick Hoult continued the firm's policy of independence, grinding and mixing their own clay bodies, mixing and fritting their own glazes, and making their own saggars. All these processes as well as the making and firing were under the supervision of the works manager, Mr L. Dixon. During World War II the supply of flints from Dieppe ceased, but an alternative supply was obtained from Ballinacurra, near Cork, in Eire.

In 1950 a nichrome belt-type tunnel kiln built by Birlec Ltd. was installed for glost firing, and in 1952 a new hardening-on tunnel by the Electric Resistance Furnace Co. Ltd., Weybridge. This provided for narrow setting, and was of the four-foot bogey type. The kiln and oven were controlled automatically, with considerable increase in production rate. By 1954 the pottery looked forward to a brightening future, but with Mr Frederick Hoult's death, interest in the ceramic side of Hoults Estates Ltd. faded, and Mr Edward Hoult permitted the storage business to occupy more and more of the pottery buildings.

The end came in 1963 with a decision to close C. T. Maling & Sons, sell the equipment, and take over the whole factory for storage. The firm's records of this period contain many sad letters offering kilns and other pieces of machinery

C. T. Maling & Sons. Beer mug stamped with Edward VII excise mark; ash tray marked m79, Deuchar's whiskey water jug, marked m87.

C. T. Maling & Sons. Minute model of a bathing hut, pattern number 875.

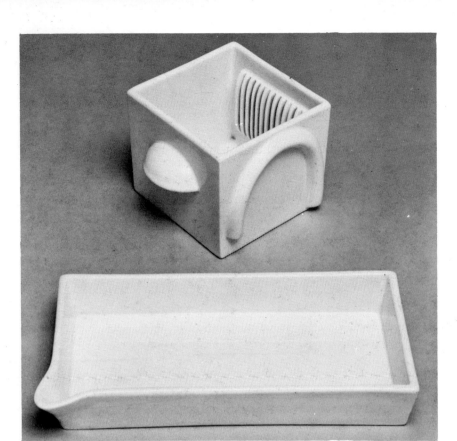

C. T. Maling & Sons. Developing tray and washing tank, stamped MALING, ENGLAND.

An advertisement published in 1927 of some of the Maling range.

C. T. Maling & Sons. Water jug, one of a
range of sizes-made for Ringtons Tea Co.,
marked m83.

C. T. Maling & Sons. Lustre-ware jug made for Ringtons Tea Co., marked m83.

Opposite.
C. T. Maling & Sons. Highly coloured rustic flower pots made for Ringtons Tea Co., marked m83.

C. T. Maling & Sons. Huge gallon tea pot made for shop window dressing, marked m87.

Cutting mug handles at Ford (B) pottery.

Flinging a ball of spread clay onto a 10 inch plate mould.

In the foreground a load is being slipped into the hardening-on kiln. In the centre background is the drawing end of a Birlec glost oven. Both were fired electrically.

The filter press room on the first floor of the slip house. In the background is a Manor press, and in the foreground a man drops clay down a chute to the de-airing pug below.

Mugs being made for the armed forces.

Decorators applying lustre to 'Springtime' ware in one of the decorating departments. Inspection by Lucien Boullemier.

C. T. Maling. Three tureens in the KILDA pattern, which was registered in 1888. (a) marked m68, (b) and (c) M58 and m68.

a

b

c

C. T. Maling. Bowl decorated with Denon's Egypt design, marked with printed letters DENON'S EGYPT and impressed 'CTM 8.89', meaning August 1889.

C. T. Maling or C. T. Maling & Sons. Tureen and stand. Keswick pattern. Impressed M58 and printed m68 with KESWICK.

C. T. Maling or C. T. Maling & Sons.
Vegetable dish with Asiatic pheasants
pattern. Impressed M58 and printed
m68.

C. T. Maling or C. T. Maling & Sons.
Side plate with Asiatic pheasants pattern.
Impressed M58, and with printed mark
similar to m24, but with the initials
'C.T.M.' The side plate is probably
earlier than the vegetable dish.

C. T. Maling & Sons. Vegetable dish in Jesmond pattern. Impressed date 1893, and printed mark m68 with JESMOND.

C. T. Maling & Sons. Vegetable dish, Blagdon pattern. Impressed M58 and printed m68 with BLAGDON. Date impressed 'SS 2.01', meaning February 1901.

C. T. Maling & Sons. Left, sauce boat with wild flower pattern, printed mark m66; right, sauce boat with Portland pattern. Marked m68 with PORTLAND. Registered in 1896.

C. T. Maling & Sons. Vegetable dish, polychrome Chang pattern. Marked similar to m71 but with CHANG instead of MOSS.

C. T. Maling & Sons. Small side plate, monochrome Chang pattern. Marked m71 but with CHANG instead of MOSS. Impressed date '12.10', meaning December 1910.

C. T. Maling & Sons. Mixing bowl marked similar to m87 but with COBBLE-STONE added.

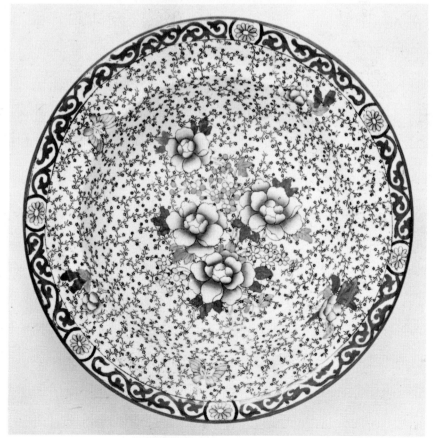

C. T. Maling and Sons. Plate with underglaze and overglaze decoration, marked m71.

C. T. Maling & Sons. Ornamented bowl
.in black, white and gold. Marked m87 in
black and gold.

C. T. Maling & Sons. Mantlepiece ornamental jars and cake stand. Blue and white
camel scene. Marked m87.

C. T. Maling & Sons. Chamber pot,
Willow pattern with gold rim. Marked
with the left half of m73.

C. T. Maling & Sons. Polychrome jumbo cup and saucer, marked m86.

C. T. Maling & Sons. Green lustre-ware flower bowl with biscuit-ware piece behind. Finished piece marked m85.

C. T. Maling & Sons. Commemorative mugs, left, marked m76 dated 1919; right, marked m69 dated 1897.

Top.
C. T. Maling & Sons. Commemorative beakers, left: dated 1935, marked with impressed '2085'; middle dated 1911, marked m72 and impressed number '2355'; right: dated 1937 and marked m88 with impressed number '2085'. (The 1935 piece is accepted as made by Maling in the absence of a firm mark since the impressed number '2085' appears on the 1935 and 1937 pieces.)

Bottom.
C. T. Maling & Sons. Other side of the three beakers seen above.

C. T. Maling & Sons. Commemorative
plate for the North East Coast Exhibition
1929, marked m81.

C. T. Maling & Sons. Commemorative ornament made for the North East Coast Exhibition 1929. Marked m81; and above the mark is:

MODEL OF THE OLD CASTLE BUILT—1080—FROM WHICH THE CITY OF NEWCASTLE ON TYNE DERIVES ITS NAME

REBUILT—1170 LAST SIEGE—1664

NORTH EAST COAST EXHIBITION MAY 1929

THE POTTERY

PRODUCING *Beautiful Creations with universal appeal*

C. T. MALING & SONS LTD
Ford Pottery · Newcastle upon Tyne

MALING ESTD. 1762

Advertisement
in the
Pottery Gazette,
November 1951,
showing the
Ford (B) pottery
from the air.

C. T. Maling & Sons (Hoults). A wall plaque marked m88. This mark was continued by Hoults for many of their cheaper wares.

C. T. Maling & Sons (Hoults). Lustreware dressing table items, marked m90.

to ceramic concerns all over the country. By 1964 Her Majesty's Inspector of Taxes was satisfied with the bills of sale, and this great company, started on Wearside in 1762, had passed into the pages of history.

Maling, John, & Co.
Stepney Terrace, Ouseburn

Mentioned in directories of 1837, 1844, 1851, 1852, 1853, 1855, 1857. In the directory of 1858 his address is given as the Old Pottery, Ouseburn. The next two directories of 1859–60, and 1861–2 merely mention Ouseburn, and the last in which his firm appears gives the address as Pottery Lane. Mr John Maling's residence was at 15 Ridley Villas.

In the Maling family tree is a John Maling, elder brother of Christopher Thompson Maling (the second of this name). This may be the John Maling of Stepney Terrace, Ouseburn.

Maling, Robert   *Ouseburn Bridge Pottery*
Ouseburn

Mentioned in directories of 1821–2, 1823, 1824, 1827–8, 1829, 1833, 1837, 1838, 1844, 1850, 1852. The 1824 directory gives his address as Ouseburn Bridge, East Ballast Hills; later entries as Ouseburn Bridge Pottery, Ouseburn.

Robert Maling transferred the family business from North Hylton on the Wear to a new pottery at Ouseburn, in 1815. The first kiln was fired on 28 June 1817. These dates are taken from a kiln book preserved at the Ford (B) Pottery which closed in 1963. The North Hylton factory was taken over by John Phillips, who also owned the Sunderland, or Garrison, Pottery, so named through its proximity to the barracks in the town. Robert brought many of the North Hylton moulds and designs to Tyneside, and it is difficult to be certain which factory produced some of the early pieces.

The Ouseburn Bridge Pottery produced general earthenwares, including printed and lustre wares. A late design appearing on Robert Maling's pieces was the High Level Bridge, built in 1849 across the Tyne at Newcastle. It carried a railway track 112 feet above the water, with a highway for stage coaches and road traffic beneath. Sometimes this bridge appeared in conjunction with views of the more famous Monkwearmouth bridge across the Wear.

Occasionally pieces of 'Gaudy Dutch' and 'Gaudy Welsh' pottery bear a Maling mark.

In 1847 Robert Maling lived at Byker Cottage. He retired in 1853 and died in 1863.

Martin, Robert, & Sons   *Railway Bridge Pottery*
Ouseburn

Mentioned in directories of 1863–4, 1865–6, 1867–8, 1869–70, 1870–1, 1871–2, 1873–4. In the first two of these directories the address is given as Pottery Lane, thereafter as Ouseburn. In the directory of 1873–4 the entry reads 'Martin, R. Jun. & Co. Ouseburn', and the same for 1874–5. In 1877 the entry is 'Martin, Robert & Co.', and the same style is retained for directories of 1877–8, 1879, and 1878–80.

Jewitt states that Robert Martin & Co. succeeded William

Blakey in 1860, though the directory entries suggest that it may have been a little later—about 1862.

McGregor, D.   *Tyne Main Pottery*
5 Folly, Gateshead

Mentioned in directories of 1852 and 1853. He succeeded R. C. Wilson.

Morris, W.   *Albion Pottery*
Ouseburn

Mentioned in directories of 1871–2, 1873–4, 1874–5. He succeeded W. Atkinson. The pottery appears to have closed in 1875.

Morrow & Parke   *Railway Bridge Pottery*
Ouseburn

This firm is not mentioned in any directory examined, but according to Jewitt it succeeded Mr George Gray about 1851–2, and was followed by Mr Rogers, who extended the buildings. Rogers is mentioned in a directory of 1857–8, and there may have been an interval between the occupancy by the two firms.

Mould & Stonehouse
Lime Street, Ouseburn

Mentioned in a directory of 1873–4, but no street number given.

Newcastle Pottery

'NEWCASTLE POTTERY' may appear as the mark on early 19th-century pieces and refers to the pottery at Skinnerburn. A directory of 1801 gives Addison, Falconer & Co., Newcastle Pottery, Skinnerburn.

The Willett Collection in the Brighton Museum contains two rare earthenware mugs marked 'Newcastle Pottery'. On one a pair of sorrowing Englishmen mourn the death of Lord Nelson at Trafalgar in 1805; the other shows the Duke of York and Mrs Clarke arranging political chicaneries to their mutual advantage (c. 1809).[19]

Among the specimens of British pottery in the Museum of Practical Geology, London, is one described in the official catalogue: 'T.3. Frog Mug, printed in black, with monument and trophies in memory of Lord Nelson; inscribed NEWCASTLE POTTERY'. This was probably made by Addison, Falconer & Co.

'Frog mugs' were also known as ague mugs. Many were made in the days when ague was common; it was believed that a sudden shock had a beneficial effect on the patient, and the appearance of a frog in one's drink was supposed to effect a cure.

A directory of 1847 gives 'Wallace, James & Co., earthenware manufacturers, *Newcastle Pottery*, Forth Banks'.

[19] These two pieces are illustrated in Godden, *An Illustrated Encyclopaedia of British Pottery and Porcelain*, p. 249.

John Maling (?). Willow pattern side plate provisionally ascribed to John Maling, marked M91.

Robert Maling. Albion pattern side plate with impressed mark M92.

Robert Maling. Comfit plate with pink oriental bird and flowers, marked M93 and m94.

Robert Maling—C. T. Maling. Willow pattern side plate marked M56 and m95. It would appear that this piece was made in 1853 when C. T. Maling was taking over the firm from his father.

Northumberland Pottery

See Bird & Co., p. 46.

Parker, Benjamin   *Carr's Hill Pottery*
Gateshead

Mentioned in a directory of 1847. He seems to have been followed by Kendall & Walker.

Patterson, George   *Sheriff Hill Pottery*
Gateshead

Mentioned in directories of 1851, 1853, 1855, 1861–2, 1867–8, 1869–70, 1870–71, 1871–2, 1873–4, 1874–5, 1877, 1877–8, 1879, 1878–80, 1881–2, 1883, 1884, 1885–6, 1887–8, 1889–90, 1891–2. The directory of 1867–8 gives a second address of Three Indian King's Court, Quayside, which was probably his exporting depot, and the directory of 1879 includes a description of his products: 'Patterson, G. (Manufacturer of C. C. sponged, painted, and printed earthenware, and all kinds of brown ware) Sheriff Hill Pottery'.

Patterson, Thomas, & Co.   *Tyne Pottery*
Felling Shore
later at **Gateshead**   *Sheriff Hill Pottery*

Mentioned in directories of 1827, 1827–8, 1828, 1829, 1837. In some directories the address is given as Tyne Pottery, Felling Shore, and in others as Tyne Pottery, Heworth Shore. These are the same pottery.

In a directory of 1847 Thomas Patterson is recorded as being at Sheriff Hill.

There are several pieces of pink lustre-ware with a simple cottage design bearing the mark M102, in the Laing Art Gallery collection. See pp. 18, 100.

Patterson, T. (2)   *Carr's Hill Pottery*
Gateshead
later at **Newcastle**   *St Anthony's Pottery*

Mentioned in directories of 1885–6, and 1887–8. A directory of 1889–90 gives the firm of Patterson & Parkinson.[20]

A directory of 1892 gives the address as 'Patterson (T) & Co., St Anthony's', as does one of 1893–4, but shortly after this the firm moved to Pottery Bank, Ouseburn. A directory of 1907–8 gives Pottery Bank; but this is the last entry, and the firm probably closed in 1908.

This T. Patterson is not to be confused with the Thomas Patterson of fifty years earlier of the Tyne Pottery, Felling Shore, and later of Sheriff Hill Pottery, in 1847.

Patterson & Codling
Sheriff Hill, Gateshead

Mentioned in a directory of 1844. The senior partner was Mr Thomas Patterson.

[20] See below.

Patterson, Dawson & Codling
Heworth Shore, Gateshead

Mentioned in directories of 1833 and 1838.

Patterson & Parkinson   *Carr's Hill Pottery*
Gateshead
later at **Newcastle**   *St Anthony's Pottery*

Mentioned in a directory of 1889–90; therefore they probably occupied the premises at Carr's Hill about a year earlier. In the 1891–2 directory the address is given as St Anthony's. About 1893 the firm became T. Patterson & Co.

Patterson & Scott   *Carr's Hill Pottery*
Gateshead

Mentioned in a directory of 1891–2. A directory of 1890 gives the firm at Carr's Hill as Patterson and Parkinson. The partnership of Patterson & Scott seems to have been short lived, and the pottery probably closed in 1893.

Patton, John   *Phoenix Pottery*
Ouseburn

Mentioned in a directory of 1844 as at East Percy Street, Low Lights, North Shields; but a directory of 1847 gives 'Patton, John. earthenware manufacturer, h. Ouseburn.'[21] He was therefore living at Ouseburn at this time, and in directories of 1850, 1852, 1853, 1855, his business address is given as Ouseburn.[22]

He was succeeded by The Phoenix Pottery Company about 1856.

Phoenix Pottery Co.
Ouseburn

Mentioned in directories of 1857–8, and 1858. They succeeded John Patton about 1856, and were followed by Bell, Cook & Co.

Pipewellgate Pottery
Gateshead

This firm served as a warehouse for the products from the Sherriff Hill Pottery.

Prudhoe Pottery

The three little wall decorations shown were probably made about 1910. Only one is signed (in brushwork). See p. 102.

[21] 'h' seems to mean 'house' in the directories.
[22] See Carr & Patton, p. 49.

George Patterson. Lustre-ware plate in purple, green and brown with a pink border, marked M96.

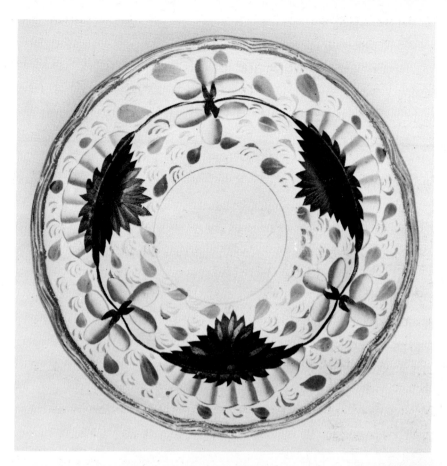

George Patterson. Part of a child's tea-set in green and mauve, marked M96.

George Patterson. Willow pattern side plate marked M96.

Thomas Patterson. Pink lustre plate, marked M102. (L.A.G.)

Thomas Patterson. Willow pattern side plate, marked M102.

Thomas Patterson (?) Willow pattern side plate, marked M103. Provisionally ascribed to Thomas Patterson after his move to Sheriff Hill.

Phoenix Pottery Company. Willow pattern side-plate, marked M104.

Prudhoe Pottery. Three small wall ornaments, hand painted. Only the top left hand piece is marked, p105.

Rawling, H.
William Street, Arthur's Hill

Mentioned in a directory of 1844.

Redhead, Wilson & Co.
Skinnerburn, Forth Bank, Newcastle

Mentioned in a directory of 1833. They may have succeeded Taylor & Son, and were followed in 1838 by J. Wallace & Co.

Robertson, William   *Tyne* or *South Shields Pottery*
South Shields

This pottery was established before 1790, as shown by the following extract from the *Chronicle*, 8 May 1790: 'South Shields Pottery to let. A tenant may be accommodated with all utensils now used for carrying on the business and a convenient warehouse situated near the river. Apply at Mr Fairle's Office, South Shields.'
In 1830 it was managed by Mr Robertson, and in 1841 it passed to Mr John Armstrong. Robson's *Commercial Directory of Durham*, 1841, however, lists 'Robertson, William, South Shield Pottery, Oyston Street'.[23]

Robinson, Gray & Burns   *Sheriff Hill Pottery*
Gateshead

This partnership succeeded M. King about 1895 and continued until Robinson's death about 1902. Gray and Burns carried on working the factory together.
Some of the workers at Sheriff Hill came from Thornaby-on-Tees. They made pottery hardware jars for Forster Blackett of Gallowgate Lead Works, and also dishes, mugs, etc., which were sold on Tyneside, especially in Blaydon and Ryton.

Rogers, E.   *Railway Bridge Pottery*
Ouseburn

Mentioned in a directory of 1857–8. He succeeded Morrow & Parke, and was followed by Mr William Blakey, who is recorded in a directory of 1858.
Mr Rogers extended the works considerably, but only seems to have been in possession of the pottery for a year or two.
An impressed mark 'ROGERS' was used by J. & G. Rogers, of Longport, Staffordshire, c. 1784–1836. The side plate illustrated seems to be of later manufacture and was bought at a house sale near Morpeth, Northumberland, together with several unmarked Willow pattern plates and side-plates, and three tureens, two marked J. BURN and the third PATTERSON. Rogers, Burn and George Patterson were all working in 1858, and it seems likely that the three pieces would have been bought about the same time and all be

from Tyneside, rather than that one would be a Staffordshire piece of at least 20 years earlier. See p. 105.

Russell, Frederick (Stone-ware)
North Shore and New-road, St Ann's

Mentioned in a directory of 1837. A directory of 1838 gives his address as Clarence Street and one of 1852 as Ouseburn. He seems to have produced stone-ware. A directory of 1841 mentions that he made brown-ware.

St Anthony's Pottery Company (later Limited)
(Nixon & Bolam)
St Anthony's and later Argyl Street, Newcastle

This small pottery started in 1949 on a piece of waste ground at St Anthony's, which gave the venture its name. The proprietors were unaware of the earlier pottery in the district. They experimented for two years with local clay from a quarry at Cowgate which supplied a brick works, and produced a rough terracotta ware. At this time Mr Nixon and Mr Bolam attended classes in pottery at King's College, University of Durham. John Howle of Jarrow started to make stone-ware, and imported ball clay from the Midlands. St Anthony's pottery began to use the same clay, and in 1951 moved to a large room over a garage in Argyl Street.
Both men were engineers, and were interested in automation as a means of cutting costs and increasing production. Apart from a few special items they abandoned throwing, and concentrated on cast ware. To reduce the number of moulds required, they added water-glass to the slurry which made it more liquid without increasing its water content, leaving less moisture for the moulds to absorb, which therefore dried quicker, and could be used again in a few minutes. Some 50 moulds produced 2,000 items a day. The use of water-glass also reduced shrinkage on drying to about a quarter of what it would have been with water alone. The handles were cast, and applied to the bodies with slip. The moulds were made of plaster of Paris.
The wares were dried for two or three days and when they were white, hard and brittle they were fired in a gas-fire kiln at 1100°C—the loading, firing, cooling, unloading and cleaning took about 36 hours. The biscuit-ware was then painted with underglaze, using commercially prepared colours, and by overlapping a wide range of hues was obtained. The company employed two girl premium apprentice potters, and five decorators, the latter carrying out swift repetitive decoration by hand; each piece varying a little from its fellows. The wares were then dipped in glaze and refired at 980°C.
St Anthony's Pottery produced numerous items of studio type, but made in quantity: jugs, vases, bowls, trays, etc.; among the key lines were mugs bearing children's names, which sold well in local department stores. Other popular pieces were piggy banks, and elephants turned on a wheel, the trunk then bent downwards, and legs, ears and tail added. They also had a contract with Celluware to produce small dishes to fit into trays made of laminated plastics.
When purchase tax rose to 50 per cent the profit margin became too small, and Mr Bolam left the firm in 1953. The company passed into voluntary liquidation in 1955.

[23] See mark m6. This may be the mark of Mr Robertson, and not of Mr Armstrong.

Sampsou, J.
Rewcastle Chare and 9 Lime Street, Ouseburn

Mentioned in a directory of 1865–6.

Schofield, James   *Ouseburn Pottery*
Stepney Square

Mentioned in a directory of 1855.

Sewell, Joseph   *St Anthony's Pottery*
Newcastle

Joseph Sewell obtained the St Anthony's Pottery from
Foster & Cutter about 1804, and produced earthenware,
cream-ware, Queen's ware, and gold, silver and pink lustre-
ware. Some of his pierced whicker baskets, and filigree
plates resembled those of Leeds, though the Tyneside
firm's were heavier pieces and of a better colour. Sewell
enjoyed a flourishing export trade to the Continent, prin-
cipally in pink lustre-ware jugs, ovoid in form with raised
vine mouldings and cupids in relief. There is a fine quintal
flower holder in the Laing Art Gallery. The best Tyneside
lustre-ware was made by this firm and its successors,
Sewell & Donkin.
    Tea services with diminutive teapots, cream jugs and cups
and saucers were a speciality of the firm. Many of these
sets have an attractive canary yellow ground colour with
silver bands at the edges. Sewell & Donkin made similar
pieces in about 1825.

Sewell & Donkin   *St Anthony's Pottery*
Newcastle

Mentioned in directories of 1821–2, 1823, 1827, 1827–8,
1828, 1833, 1837, 1838, 1844, 1850, 1851, 1852. In the following year the firm is listed as Sewell & Co. Mankowitz and
Haggar[24] illustrate a piece dated 1819, and impressed
'SEWELLS & DONKIN'. Note that this is two years before the
earliest mention of the firm in the directory of 1821. It
would appear that Joseph Sewell probably retired in 1819.
This is earlier than suggested by previous authors. Note also
the second 'S' in Sewells & Donkin. Later this seems to have
been changed to 'SEWELL & DONKIN'.

Sewell & Co.   *St Anthony's Pottery*
Newcastle

Mentioned in directories of 1853, 1855, 1857–8, 1858,
1859–60, 1861–2, 1863–4, 1865–6, 1867–8, 1869–70, 1870–1,
1871–2, 1873–4, 1874–5, 1877, 1877–8. They succeeded Sewell
& Donkin, and finally closed in 1878. The directory of
1865–6 gives an additional address to St Anthony's; namely
'Office, Printing Court Buildings'; and the directory of
1867–8, 'Printing Court Buildings, Akenside Hill, T. J.
Stevenson, Manager'. See Addendum, p. 148.

---

[24] W. Mankowitz and R. G. Haggar, *The Concise Encyclopædia
of English Pottery and Porcelain*, London, André Deutsch, 1957,
plate 71.

Sill, Thomas   *Heworth Shore Pottery*
Gateshead

There is a brief note in the *Advertiser*, 9 May 1795: 'To be
sold, by order of the Assignees of Thomas Sill, a bankrupt,
the pottery at Heworth-shore.'

Smith & Co.
Folly Wharf

Mentioned in directories of 1827–8, and 1829.

Smith, Harvey, & Co.
near Stepney

Mentioned in a directory for Newcastle and Gateshead,
1782–4.

Spearman & Co   *Skinnerburn Pottery*
Forth Banks, Newcastle

Mentioned in a directory of 1787 as 'Spearman & Co.,
Skinnerborn [*sic*] Pottery, Firthbanks' [*sic*].
    The *Journal*, 16 September 1758, carries the news item:
'On Wednesday night the Pot-house at the Skinner-Burn
was burnt down; and but for the timely assistance of the
glassmen in all likelihood many of the adjacent buildings
would have been consumed.'
    In 1787 there was a new pottery on the site, and the
Courant, 23 June 1787, reported: 'Andrew Wilson, hired
servant to Mr George Spearman and Co., Skinnerburn
Pottery, near Newcastle, did absent himself from his
master's service.'
    Three years later the pottery passed into the possession of
Addison, Falconer & Co., who controlled it for many years.

Tate, John   *Ballast Hills Pottery*

Mentioned in a directory of 1844.

Taylor & Son   *Tyne Pottery*
Felling Shore   and later at *Newcastle Pottery*

Mentioned in a directory of 1827. They appear to have
succeeded Tyler & Co. In 1827 they transferred their
business to the Newcastle Pottery, Skinnerburn, and a
directory of 1829 lists them as Taylor & Son, Newcastle
Pottery, Forth Bank.

Thompson, Thomas & Joseph   *Ouseburn Pottery*
Newcastle

Mentioned in directories of 1827, 1828–9, 1829, 1833, 1838,

F. Rogers. Willow pattern side plate, marked M106.

St Anthony's Pottery (2). Leaf plate, jug and vase, marked p108, p107 and p110 respectively. (R.B.)

St Anthony's Pottery (1). Cream-ware plate with filigree edge, marked M112. This mark is usually attributed to Joseph Sewell, but may have belonged to one of the earlier proprietors of the pottery.

Joseph Sewell. Blue and white castle pattern side plate, marked M113.

Joseph Sewell. Cream-ware filigree oval plate, marked M114. (L.A.G.)

Sewell & Donkin. Green and white jug marked '1845'. The impressed mark is M114 belonging to Joseph Sewell. Either, an obsolete mark was used; or old biscuit-ware was decorated several years after its manufacture.

Sewell & Donkin. Small black and white saucer, marked M116.

Sewell & Donkin. Large round Willow pattern bread plate, marked M115.

Tuer, James, & Co.
Ouseburn

Mentioned in a directory of 1824.

Turnbull, G. R.
16 and later 14 Stepney Street, Ouseburn

Mentioned in directories of 1863–4, 1865–6, 1867, 1867–8, 1870–1, 1871–2, 1873–4, 1874–5. The change from 16 to 14 Stepney Street appears in the directory of 1870–1, and probably indicates a move in the previous year. Alternatively it may only indicate a renumbering of the buildings in the street.

Turpin & Co.   *Ouseburn Pottery*

Mentioned in a directory of 1841.

Tyler & Co.   *Tyne Pottery*
Newcastle

Mentioned in directories for 1821–3, the firm appears to have been succeeded by Taylor & Son.

Walker, C.
7 Lime Street, Ouseburn

Mentioned in directories of 1855, 1857–8, 1858, 1859–60.

Walker, Cuthbert Kendle
138 Headlam Street, Byker

Mentioned in a directory of 1883. His name is then missing from the directories of the next four years, appearing again in 1887, but with the address Foundry Lane, Ouseburn. He is listed in this way in directories of 1887–8, 1888, 1889–90, 1891–2, and 1892.

Walker, John Hedley
Pottery Lane, Ouseburn

Mentioned in directories of 1865–6, 1867–8, 1869–70, 1871–2, 1873–4, 1874–5, 1877, 1879, 1878–80, 1881–2, 1883, 1883–4, 1885–6. The directory of 1879 gives his address as Foundry Lane, Ouseburn, and he appears to have transferred from Pottery Lane about this time.

Jewitt[25] says he obtained the premises in Pottery Lane in 1860, and that he produced flower-pots, chimney-pots, and horticultural vessels of various kinds, as well as lead-pots and lead-dishes for use in neighbouring lead-works.

---

[25] Jewitt, op. cit.

Wallace & Co.
Pottery Road, Forth Banks

Mentioned in directories of 1858, 1859–60, 1861–2, 1863–4, 1865–6, 1867–8, 1869–70, 1870–1, 1871–2. The directory of 1870–1 gives the address as Pottery Lane, Ouseburn, and this address continues for directories of 1873–4, 1877, 1879, 1878–80, 1880, 1881–2, 1883, 1884, 1885–6, 1887, 1887–8, 1888, 1889–90, 1890, 1891–2, 1892. A directory of 1893–4 gives the address as Foundry Lane, Ouseburn, and Kelley's directory of 1902 as 7 Lime Street. This is the last time the firm is mentioned; it is missing in Ward's directory of 1903–4.

The directory of 1885–6 lists 'Wallace & Co., flower pots, W.C. basins and traps, chimney tops, etc. Pottery Lane'.

Wallace & Co. succeeded James Wallace and Co. in 1858 at the pottery in Forth Banks, and transferred their business in 1870 to Pottery Lane, Ouseburn. They appear to have given up making tableware and ceramics and concentrated on producing flower pots and sanitary wares. An advertisement card belonging to this period is illustrated.

Wallace, James, & Co   *Newcastle Pottery*
Forth Banks

Mentioned in directories of 1838, 1844, 1847, 1850, 1851, 1852, 1853, 1855, 1857–8. Before 1838 the pottery was managed by Redhead, Wilson & Co., and James Wallace & Co. were succeeded by Wallace & Co.

Wallace, Robert

Mentioned in a directory of 1847. His residence was at 86 Blenheim Street, Newcastle, and as the same address is given under Wallace, James, & Co., earthenware manufacturers, Robert Wallace would seem to have been one of the partners in the firm, possibly the '& Co.' recorded on the mug in the author's collection. See pp. 111, 146.

Wallace, T.
Forth Banks

Mentioned in a directory of 1877–8.

Wallace, Thomas, & Son
Castle Stairs and Warburton Place, Gateshead

Mentioned in directories of 1827, 1828, 1828–9, 1833, and 1838. The 1828 directory gives the address as Carr Hill. Two directories of 1837 give the address as Forth Bank and Skinnerburn respectively, suggesting that the firm moved there about 1836. The 1838 entry gives the address as Castle Stairs and Warburton Place; this may be an error, or perhaps the firm returned for a short time to its original premises.

Wardhaugh, H.
Back Lane

Mentioned in directories of 1873–4 and 1874–5.

G. R. Turnbull. Albion pattern side plate, marked M119. (L.A.G.)

Wallace & Co. Advertisement card giving Pottery Lane, Forth Bank address.

Top.
Wallace & Co. Willow pattern side plate,
marked M120 with printed mark OPAQUE
CHINA within a floral border (not illustrated).

Bottom.
View of Newcastle showing the Forth
Bank Pottery (arrowed) Watercolour by
J. W. Carmichael. (L.A.G.)

James Wallace & Co. Lustre-ware burial
mug, 1857, marked m124.

Warburton, Ellen   *Warburton Place Pottery*
Carr's Hill, Gateshead

She succeeded Isaac Warburton in the business. The factory manufactured earthenware of 'various sorts'. This probably included high-class wares. The factory closed in 1817, apart from a small portion occupied by other proprietors.[26]

Warburton, Isaac   *Warburton Place Pottery*
Carr's Hill

By 1795 this pottery was owned by Isaac Warburton, who succeeded John Warburton. Between 1801 and 1811 the business passed to Ellen Warburton. The following appeared in the *Chronicle*, 19 September 1795: 'Run-away from his master's service Henry Donnison, indentured apprentice to Isaac Warburton, of Warburton-Place, Earthen-Ware Manufacturer.'

Warburton, John   *Pandon Dean* and
Carr's Hill   *Warburton Place Pottery*

He is mentioned in directories of 1778, 1787, and 1790. John Warburton opened a pottery at Pandon Dean about 1730, making brown-ware and about 1740 founded a pottery at Carr's Hill. This was the first in the district to make 'white wares'. The *Chronicle*, of 28 October 1769 records: 'John Warburton, at his Earthen Warehouse on the Quay, Newcastle...', and in the *Chronicle*, 19 May 1770: '... of John Warburton, the Quay, Newcastle, may be had for Exportation, etc., various sorts of Earthenware of his own manufacture.'

John Warburton was in partnership with William Tyrer for a time, but this was dissolved in 1774, when the *Chronicle* announced on 14 May: 'William Tyrer, Potter, having declined business in favour of John Warburton; the said John Warburton sells various sorts of Earthenware of his own Manufacture at his shop on the Keyside, a few doors below his old shop.' By 1795 the pottery had passed to Isaac Warburton.

Among the Willett Collection in the Brighton Museum is a cream-ware teapot decorated with a print showing a rural scene and three pheasants. At the bottom of the design is written 'J. WARBURTON, N. C. TYNE.' This was probably the work of John Warburton, or Joseph Warburton (see below).

Warburton, Joseph

Mentioned in the *Journal*, 12 February 1757:
> Whereas Joseph Warburton has been employed for some years in making China at Bow near London. He does hereby make known to the publick that he finds better materials here for the purpose, and to be had at a cheaper rate. Therefore any gentleman willing to encourage such an undertaking may know particulars of the expense by applying to the above Joseph Warburton at Mr Hilcot's [*sic*] Pot-house on the South Shore.

Warburton, Joseph
Heworth Shore, Gateshead

Mentioned in a directory of 1833.

Wilson, C.
Low Teams

Mentioned in a directory of 1851.

Wilson, Edward & Robert   *Ballast Hills Pottery*
East Ballast Hills, Ouseburn

Mentioned in directories of 1821–2, 1823, 1824, 1827, 1828–9, 1829, and 1833. The directory entry in 1827 gives the additional information that they made black, brown, yellow and figured wares.

Wilson, Robert Christopher   *Tyne Main Pottery*
Salt Meadows, Gateshead

Mentioned in directories of 1844, 1847, 1850, 1851, and 1852. In 1847 he had premises at Friars Goose, and a residence at 106 High Street, Gateshead. He seems to have had a warehouse at Folly Wharf on the quay.

Wilson, William
St Anthony's, East Ballast Hills

Mentioned in directories of 1824 and 1837. He made brown-ware.

Wood, John
Heworth Shore, Gateshead

The first reference appears to be in the *Table Book*[27]: 'A fire broke out in the earthenware manufactory of Mr Wood, at Heworth Shore, near Gateshead, and the whole building, apart from Mr Wood's dwelling-house, was reduced to ashes. Several cottages surrounding the pottery were also burnt down.'

He is mentioned in directories of 1824, 1827, 1828–9, 1829 and 1837.

Wood, John, & Co.   *Stepney Pottery*
Stepney Bank, Ouseburn

Mentioned in directories of 1877, 1879, 1878–80, 1880, 1881–2, 1883, 1883–4, 1884, 1885–6, 1887, 1887–8, 1888, 1889–90, 1890, 1891–2, 1892, 1893–4, 1898, 1901–2, 1909–10 and 1912.

The directory of 1879 carried an advertisement: 'John Wood Stepney Pottery, Newcastle-on-Tyne. Manufacturer of

---

[26] Jewitt, op. cit.

[27] Richardson, op. cit., reference of 7 March 1822.

R. C. Wilson. Small black and white plate, 'A Present for William', marked M125. Provisionally ascribed to R. C. Wilson.

John Wood, Stepney Pottery. Albion pattern vegetable dish. Marks M126 and M130.

John Wood, Stepney Pottery. Classical pattern side plate, marked M126 and m130. (L.A.G.)

John Wood, Stepney Pottery. Oriental pattern side plate, marked M126 and m129.

white and coloured, and every description of brown earthenware. For home and Export.' The directory of 1883 gave the address as 36 Stepney Street.

An advertisement in the directory of 1888 referred to 'J. Wood, Stepney Pottery. Manufacturer of every description of earthenware, also gas reflectors, and lamp tops'. In 1892 the firm became a limited company. The last entry in 1912 is: 'Wood, J. & Co. Ltd. Stepney Bank'. See Addendum, p. 148.

Wood, Joseph
Felling Shore, Gateshead

Mentioned in directories of 1827, 1828, 1833, 1837, and 1838. The directories of 1828 and 1833 list him as 'grocer and earthenware manufacturer, Felling shore, Gateshead'.

Yellowley, Robert
Ouseburn

Mentioned in a directory of 1801. He took over the pottery from Hillcoat, Brown and Backhouse, and was succeeded by T. & J. Thompson.

Above.
John Wood, Stepney Pottery. Brown slipware baking dish, marked M127.

Opposite.
(*top*) Fell & Co. Wild Rose pattern side plate, marked M37.
(*bottom*) Fell & Co. Chinese scene on a side plate marked M37.

Young, G. S.
14 Charlotte Street, South Shields

Mentioned in a directory of 1874–5.

Young, J.
Lime Street, Ouseburn

Mentioned in directories of 1887, 1887–8, and 1888.

116

Appendices

1

The Maling Family

The Maling family, originally Huguenot refugees, settled in Scarborough, and in about 1688 William Maling gave the Valley Gardens to the town, with £10,000 to lay them out. He had 12 children, one of whom, William, went to Sunderland in 1723, and in 1740 married Catherine, daughter of Christopher Thompson, of Hendon Lodge, Sunderland. In 1743 he purchased the Woodhouse estate at North Hylton, and in 1762 founded the Hylton Pot-works for his two sons whom he installed to run the factory. The elder, Christopher Thompson Maling (1741–1810) was aged 20, and the younger, John (1746–1823) was 16. Christopher studied for the Bar at Cambridge and had a brilliant academic career. John became a partner in the Sunderland Banking House of Russell, Allan, Maling & Wade, which was established in 1787, in addition to his interest in the Hylton Pot-works.

John's son, Robert Maling (1781–1863) entered the pottery at the age of 16. In 1815 he transferred the business to Tyneside, the first kiln at the new Ouseburn Bridge Pottery being fired on 28 June 1817. These premises passed to Robert's son, Christopher Thompson Maling (1824–1901) (the second of this name) in 1853. Robert Maling died in 1863.

Christopher Thompson Maling built the Ford pottery which was opened in 1859, and sold the old Ouseburn Bridge Pottery to the Bell Brothers, who re-named it the Albion, presumably after Albion Street in which it stood.

In 1879 C. T. Maling extended his empire by building the huge New Ford Pottery at Walker, known as the (B) factory, distinguishing it from the Ford (A) Pottery in Ford Street, Ouseburn. These Ford factories should not be confused with the earlier Low Ford Pottery on the south bank of the Wear, built on land owned by the Maling family and leased to Mr Dawson. This concern was also known as Dawson's Pottery. It was situated across the river from the original Maling Hylton Pot-works, later renamed the North Hylton Pottery by John Phillips who bought it from Robert Maling in 1817.

In 1889 C. T. Maling took his three sons, John Ford Maling (1858–1924), Christopher Thompson Maling (1863–1934) (the third of this name), and Frederick Theodore Maling (1866–1937) into partnership, the firm becoming C. T. Maling & Sons.

C. T. Maling senior retired in 1899 and died in 1901, the firm being carried on by his sons. Mr John Ford Maling managed the Ford (A) Pottery; and Messrs C. T. and F. T. Maling the Ford (B) Pottery in Walker.

Mr Frederick Theodore Maling's son, Christopher Thompson Maling (the fourth of this name), entered the business in 1929, and apart from the years of World War II, remained with the company until it was sold to Hoults Estates Ltd. in 1947. Mr C. T. Maling is now connected with the glass industry. The following extracts are taken from a letter written by him, 8 July 1969:

Malings were completely self sufficient apart from the raw materials. They blunged the Ball and China clays from Devon and Cornwall, crushed and ground the Cornwall Stone, and calcined, crushed and ground the flint stones. They made their own glaze from Borax, Whiting, Lead, etc. They made their own fireclay 'Saggars' (containers in which to fire the pots in bottle ovens); they made their own crates and casks for packing. In addition they had their own designers, among whom were Toft, Miguet, and Boullemier, modeller, mould makers (plaster of Paris), and copper plate engraver (for transfer prints). They had their own electro-plating shop, joiner's shop, fitter's shop, blacksmith's shop, and at one time, made their own lithograph sheets from stones. They also had bricklayers to repair the kilns, etc. . . .

After C.T. the second died, between 1901–30, four of his children, who were not in the business, were bought out, necessitating in some cases, heavy mortgages being taken out on the property . . .

At the end of the war only about half the premises was being used for manufacturing, and as Hoults were badly in need of storage space, they made an offer for the land, buildings and firm.

I was the only member of the family in the business, which was still in the hands of the trustees (in fact F.T.'s widow is still living). I, with some others, tried unsuccessfully to raise the finance to purchase Malings, so it went to Hoults. Hindsight tells me that I should have managed somehow to buy the place.

Maling's Last Shed

When the author visited the Ford Furniture Repository [Ford (B) Pottery] in August 1968, all the buildings had been taken over for storage except for one long low red brick shed, whose slate roof leaked in many places and weather-beaten door hung half open. There were no windows; the only light coming from the open doorway and the holes in the roof; but in the semi-darkness rows of shelving extended from the floor to the ceiling loaded with thousands of plaster moulds, pieces of biscuit-ware, white-ware, and occasional coloured items, all covered with a thick layer of soot. The floor and walls were damp with rainwater, and there was a dank smell of rotting wood.

Plans for clearing this pattern shed and converting it into a furniture store had been delayed through lack of staff, and thus the author was given the opportunity to rescue some of the material awaiting destruction. There was so much in the shed, and time was so short, that the rescue procedure resembled a robbery at a department store, grabbing whatever took the fancy.

The shelves were numbered from 260 to 540, and each section contained a particular type of ware, plates being together, as were dishes, medical wares, bedpans, urinals, sanitary ware, cups, mugs, teapots, vases, bowls, etc.; but this orderly arrangement was frequently upset by unrelated objects which had been thrust into any vacant space. It also seemed as if the shed had been visited before, when no doubt, the choicest pieces had been culled from the shelves.

Every item had been labelled, though many of these were indecipherable through damp, or had dropped off and been lost; but legible labels remained where one article had been stored inside another, or on plates, saucers and dishes in the centre of a stack.

Three car loads of pottery were removed from the shed and many weekends were spent in cleaning the pieces, deciphering labels still legible, and recording marks.

Two types of inhalers, that on the left marked m88, that on the right back stamped.

G. MAW SON & SONS LTD.
LONDON & BARNET

(M.L.S.)

Traveller's miniature slipper bed-pan back-stamped 's. MAW SON & SONS, LONDON, ENGLAND Rᵈ Nº 116628' (registered in 1888); bedside phlegm-pot, no mark; ointment jar, no mark; and child's feeding cup, mark M60. (M.L.S.)

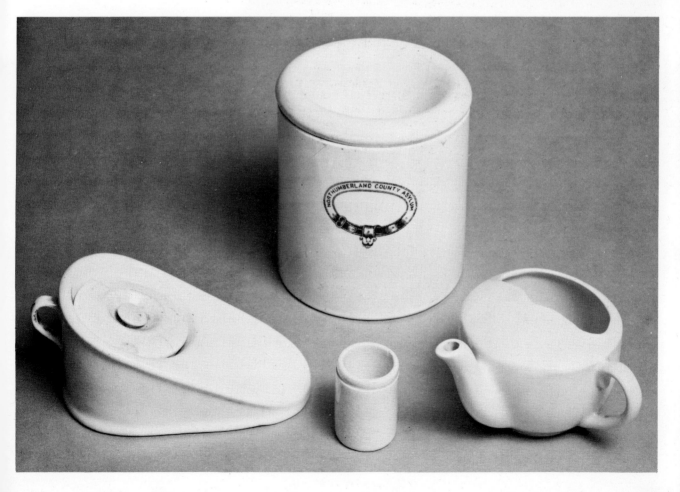

Opposite and left.
Earthenware stacked on the shelves in Maling's last shed, August 1968.

Maling's last shed seen from outside. See also p. 93. This pattern-shed is seen behind the middle chimney.

Biscuit-ware, glazed, and finished ointment pot, unmarked. (M.L.S.)

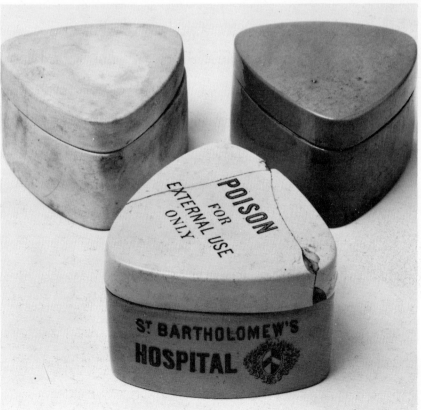

POISON
FOR
EXTERNAL USE
ONLY

ST BARTHOLOMEW'S
HOSPITAL

Ointment jar and its plaster mould, impressed '$\frac{1}{4}$'. (M.L.S.)

Sketch of the layout of the Maling Ford (B) Pottery when taken over by Hoults in 1947.

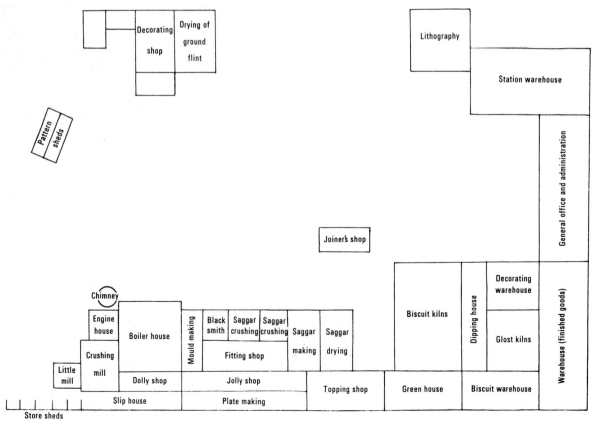

White-ware plate marked M58, and sweet
dish marked m76.   (M.L.S.)

White-ware mug, marked in print MADE IN ENGLAND, teapot, marked m88, and mug, no mark. (M.L.S.)

Unknown white-ware object 22 inch high, marked M58. (M.L.S.)

White oval plate with royal cypher of
Edward VII. Marked M58 and impressed
'S.P. 10.07' (October 1907), and m68
with addition of:
C. T. MALING & SONS
NEWCASTLE ON TYNE
1907
(Note that printed mark '1907' agrees with
impressed mark of 10.07.)

Jelly mould and shortbread trays, the latter
in biscuit state and unmarked, the former
marked M58.   (M.L.S.)

2

The Willow Pattern

Until 1842 there was no protection against piracy of ceramic designs, and by 1865 nearly 200 firms had produced their own versions of the Willow pattern. Early pieces are a soft cobalt blue; later a hard indigo was used. Pink, red, purple and green pieces are not earlier than mid-Victorian; 18th-century Willow ware was light in weight, well-moulded, and carefully printed. Some of the 19th-century work was very carelessly done, and the items weigh heavily. Dappling is a sign of age. If a piece is examined in an oblique light the surface of the glaze looks like smooth sea-sand after a heavy shower of rain, or the skin of an orange. This effect is not found on pieces made after 1830. Victorian Willow pattern has a chalky whiteness, easily differentiated from the faint creamy colour of pieces made in previous reigns.

All Tyneside Willow pattern is 19th- or 20th-century. The earliest piece seen by the author is a side plate made by Thomas Patterson at the Tyne Pottery about 1828, and exhibiting well-marked 'dappling'.

Reference books describe variations in the number of apples on the tree behind the house in the designs of different firms. Davenport's Willow pattern has only 25 apples on dinner plates; Adams 32 apples before 1805 and 52 apples after this date. Copeland made a large quantity of Willow pattern ware between 1835 and 1856 with 31 apples on the tree.

The results of examining pieces of Tyneside Willow pattern are recorded in the table below. The apples on some designs are easy to count, but in others there are varying degrees of superimposition and it may be doubtful how many apples are depicted.

Number of apples in different potters' versions of the Willow pattern

Firm	Date	Piece	Tiers	No. of apples
I. & T. Bell	c. 1860	dinner plate	3	38
J. Burns	c. 1855	soup plate	4	33
John Carr	c. 1845	side plate	4	38
T. Fell & Co.	c. 1840	side plate	4	32
T. Fell & Co.	c. 1850	side plate	3	32
T. Fell & Co.	c. 1850	meat server	3	33
Galloway & Atkinson	c. 1863	dinner plate	3	37
C. T. Maling	c. 1855	side plate	3	40
C. T. Maling	c. 1860	side plate	4	32
C. T. Maling	c. 1865	side plate	4	32
C. T. Maling	c. 1870	side plate	3	55
C. T. Maling	c. 1890	entrée dish	3	33
C. T. Maling	c. 1930	bowl	4	39
John Maling	c. 1855	side plate	4	50
Patterson & Co.	c. 1828	side plate	3	52
Phoenix Co.	c. 1857	side plate	3	52
Phoenix Co.	c. 1857	side plate	3	57
Sewell & Donkin	c. 1840	round cake plate	4	36
Wallace & Co.	c. 1865	dinner plate	4	29
Wallace & Co.	c. 1865	side plate	4	46

The Willow pattern was wholly western in concept, though based on designs found on Chinese blue and white porcelain. Possibly to help sales, a romantic legend was invented, taken from the English poem, *Lord Ullen's Daughter*, the tragic ending being changed to a happy one.

Once upon a time a Chinese mandarin of high degree lived in a pagoda behind a strong fence and under the branches of a large apple tree. Nearby a weeping willow hung over the river. This nobleman had a very beautiful daughter named Kong-Shee, whom he had promised in marriage to an old but wealthy merchant, Tan-Jin. The girl, however, had fallen in love with her father's secretary, Chang, whom she met in secret and to whom she had sworn eternal fidelity. When her father discovered these meetings he dismissed Chang from his service and threatened him with a lingering death, while he imprisoned his erring daughter in her room overhanging the river until she should promise to forget her lover and marry the elderly merchant.

As the arrangements for the wedding were hurried on Kong-Shee wept in the solitude of her prison. One day half a coconut shell came floating past her window bearing a love letter from Chang. He mourned their cruel fate and declared that life without her was worthless, and that if she married another he would commit suicide.

In her reply Kong-Shee proclaimed her devotion and told her lover that he must gather the fruit he coveted (herself) when the willow blossom was dropping on the bough. This hint gave him the approximate date of the wedding.

The wedding-day arrived, and with it Chang, an interloper among the numerous guests. Chang saw his sweetheart and persuaded her to elope with him; but the girl's absence was discovered at once, and as the pair were crossing the bridge her father almost caught them. These are the three figures on the bridge; Kong-Shee is carrying a distaff, emblem of her virginity; Chang a box containing her jewels; and the pursuing father a whip.

The lovers found a temporary hiding place in the small house at the end of the bridge, and signalled to the little boat on the water to take them to Chang's home in the upper portion of the design; but the angry father noticed them and knocked down the door, intending to beat them to death with his whip.

At this moment of danger, the gods intervened to save the lovers, and changed them into turtle doves, which can be seen flying in company from the paternal vengeance. They lived happily ever after.

Ten Tyneside Willow pattern side plates are illustrated. Note the difference in the birds, and in the various apple trees. On careful study many other curious modifications will be noticed. See pp. 51, 62, 97, 100–2, 105, 108, 111, 117.

Persian blue pattern on an oval plate, marked M58 and m67, with impressed mark '1897'. (M.L.S.)

Opposite.

Brosely pattern loving-cup, marked m87, and a biscuit-ware prototype marked '20/5/1931' on the side. (The latter from M.L.S.)

Eslington pattern single and double handled mugs, marked m68 and ESLINGTON. (M.L.S.)

Bowl and jar of Brosely pattern, plate of persian blue. The plate is marked M58 and m68, and impressed date 9.02 (September 1902). The other two pieces are unmarked. (M.L.S.)

Brosely pattern cake plate, marked m78. (M.L.S.)

3

The Pottery Industry on Tyneside in 1889

The British Association's *Handbook to the Industries of Newcastle and District*, 1889, gives an interesting insight into the ceramic industry on Tyneside at this time, in two short articles by Henry Heath and Christopher Thompson Maling:

In January 1849 workmen making the entrance to the South Dock, Sunderland, unearthed the remains of a Roman pottery 8 ft below the surface. It was in the form of a circle 29 ft in diameter, hewn out of the limestone rock. Four perfect Roman bottles and a quantity of red and yellow ochre were found.

Pottery of the North East has only reached mediocrity; even as far back as the Roman Occupation; and subsequently to that of the Saxons, when in neither case were the productions of this district approaching in excellence those of the Midlands and Southern Counties.

In ancient times when only local clays were used, the reason was simple—the district possessed none of the clays, rich in colour and fine in grain equal·to those in the finely linigated beds from the Devonian strata of some of the southern and western counties; hence the superior pottery of the Romans found at Upchurch, Castor and Cleveland, etc., where the manufacture was carried on, apparently under one management, to an extent unparalleled in modern enterprise.

From Roman times until 1686 when Dr Plot published his *Natural History of the County of Stafford*, little improvement or change had been made in the potter's art; but at that time the introduction of stoneware, Dutch stoneware and Delft stimulated experimentation. These crude efforts are to be seen in the productions of Thomas and Ralph Toft, and A. Sands. Up to this period these Staffordshire potters had only local clays to rely on: but shortly after this period 'foreign clays'—shale clays from Devon and Dorset—were discovered, and their use enabled vast improvements to be made.

During the last twenty years [1869–1889] many north-eastern potteries have closed; but the size of the remainder has increased, and the total turnover has remained about constant. The consumption of the local brown clay, however, fell greatly, and the introduction of machinery reduced the labour force quite considerably. When the six potteries in Northumberland (1889) are in full work not more than 700 hands are employed; but some 14,000 tons of white clay are used annually, and about 1,000 tons of local clay for making brown-ware. Some 35,000 tons of coal is burnt annually.

The local production of domestic pottery for home consumption, and for export to traditional overseas markets (mainly Scandinavia and North America) holds its own against Staffordshire and any other district in the United Kingdom.

4

John Carr and the Low Lights Pottery

The author is indebted to Mrs Margaret Bell for the following information about the John Carr family and the Low Lights Pottery extracted from the 1841, 1851 and 1861 censuses of North Shields.

1841   John Carr, æt. 35; Margaret, his wife, æt. 32; Thomas, æt. 6; Robert, æt. 3; and one servant.

1851   John Carr, æt. 45, living at East Percy St.; he employed 65 men, 32 women, 26 boys, 22 girls.

1861   John Carr, æt. 55, born at Sheriff Hill, Gateshead; master brewer and earthenware manufacturer, employing 56 men, 15 women, 20 boys.
Thomas Carr, æt. 25, born N. Shields; earthenware manufacturer.
Robert Carr, æt. 22, born N. Shields; earthenware manufacturer.
Arnold Carr, æt. 13, born N. Shields; scholar.
Joseph Carr, æt. 11, born N. Shields; scholar.

There were two servants living in the house at 1 Walker Place, North Shields.

A Directory of Cumberland, Westmorland, Northumberland and Durham of 1858 gives 'John Carr and Sons, 21 Norfolk Street, and Low Lights Pottery, North Shields; and Carr, Ormston & Carr, Brewers, Maltsters & Wholesale wine and spirit merchants. Offices 20 Norfolk Street, and Low Lights Brewery'.

The points to note are that John Carr was born in 1806 at Sheriff Hill, Gateshead (where there was a pottery) and by 1841 was living in North Shields. By 1851 he was employing 147 workers, and by 1861 this had declined to 91 workers. At this time two of his sons had joined him as pottery manufacturers. In 1858 John Carr and one of the sons were partners in a brewery at Low Lights with offices next to those of the pottery in Norfolk Street.

The censuses also give a few details of some of the workpeople in the pottery:

1841   Aaron Ryles, æt. 25, not born in Northumberland; Isabella Ryles, his wife, born in Northumberland; Sarah, æt. 4, born in North Shields.

1841   Daniel Ryles, æt. 42, a pottery engraver, not born in Northumberland; Betsey, his wife, æt. 47, not born in Northumberland; Betsey, æt. 7, not born in Northumberland.

1841   John Fotheringham, æt. 15, working in the pottery. He was still there as a potter in 1851.

1851   John Ryles, æt. 47, a pot-painter, born at Prestonpans (where there was a pottery); Jane Ryles, his wife, born in Whitley, Northumberland; Margaret, æt. 19, born in South Shields (where there was a pottery); Elizabeth, æt. 14, born in North Shields; John, æt. 10, born in North Shields.

1851   George Royles, æt. 51, pot-painter (not in the 1841 census); Michael Royles, æt. 20, his son, pot-painter; Margaret, æt. 19 and Maria, æt. 13, both employed in the pottery rubbing ware.

1851   Michael Ryals, æt. 35, born in Chester, Staffordshire. Engraver in pottery. Unmarried.

1851   John Mather, æt. 52, born in Gateshead, potter; Sarah, æt. 56, his wife, born in Gateshead; Alan, æt. 25, his son, born in Sandgate, Newcastle; Thomas, æt. 14, potter's apprentice and born in North Shields.

1851   Edward Hogg, æt. 35, born in Gateshead; Ann Hogg, æt. 30, born in Sunderland; Jane, æt. 14, born in Sunderland (there were potteries at Sunderland); May, æt. 8, born at Hylton, scholar (there was a pottery at Hylton); Christina, æt. 6, born at Hylton, scholar; Isabella, æt. 4, born at North Shields; Edward, æt. 2, born at North Shields; Janet, æt. 2 months, born at North Shields.

1861   Thomas Mather, æt. 25, pot-painter. (His father, John Mather, worked in the pottery in 1851 but is not mentioned in 1861).

These details from the census figures show how the pottery at North Shields recruited its staff from other pottery centres, both on Tyneside, and from Wearside, Prestonpans in Scotland, and from Staffordshire. The Hogg family are particularly interesting. The father was born in Gateshead, and probably trained there as a potter, moving to Sunderland where he met his wife, and their first child Jane was born in that town. Then the family moved to Hylton, where May and Christina were born, and finally they settled in North Shields, having three more children there.

Opposite.
C. T. Maling. A pair of vases made in an Urbino style for an exhibition in London in 1881. Said to be unique. Only one vase is marked, with p65.

Over page.
Sewell & Donkin. Pink lustre-ware vase but marked M114 which belonged to Joseph Sewell. By 1826 the factory wa owned by Sewell and Donkin. (L.A.G.

Registration Marks found on Tyneside Pottery

All known marks on Tyneside pieces are illustrated on the following pages. They are listed alphabetically under the names of the potteries on whose products they are found.

Printed and painted marks were photographed; impressed and incised marks were accurately drawn. For the method of classification, see the last paragraph on page 4.

All the marks are reproduced at approximately life-size, except for the following, where the proportion of the actual size is indicated in parentheses: M1, M2, M3 ($\times 2$); M6, m27 ($\times \frac{1}{2}$); M31 ($\times \frac{3}{4}$); m32, m68, m76 ($\times 2$); m81 ($\times \frac{1}{2}$); m85, m88 ($\times 2$); M127 ($\times \frac{3}{8}$).

Readers may like to add marks they discover themselves in the columns below.

ADAMSEZ Ltd.

M1 Impressed mark of Moses J. Adams, used between 1904 and 1914. Impressed numbers occurring with it refer to the glazes. See p. 43.

M2 Found on Adamesk ware. (L.A.G.)

M3 Impressed, but with print in the depths of the impression. See p. 44 (L.A.G.)

M4 Impressed mark found on Elanware. See p. 45. (L.A.G.)

M5 Impressed mark of Alan H. Adams. See p. 45. (L.A.G.)

ARMSTRONG, John, & Co.

m6 Printed mark on the side of a mug. See pp. 45 and 102. (L.A.G.)

(BAGSHAW, J.)

m7 After this book went to press, m7, a mark once attributed to a Tyneside potter, possibly J. Bagshaw, was found to be definitely not from Tyneside, and remains unidentified.

BARKER, H.

m8 Printed signature beneath the decoration on a mug. See p. 47. (L.A.G.)

BELL, Isaac, & GALLOWAY and ATKINSON

m9 Printed mark of Isaac Bell & Galloway and Atkinson. Found on a Willow pattern plate together with the impressed mark of Galloway and Atkinson (M54).

BELL, Isaac, & Thomas

m10 Printed mark of Isaac & Thomas Bell. Found on a Willow pattern plate, together with impressed mark M11.

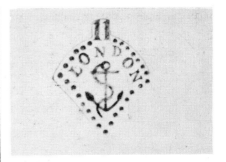

M11 Impressed mark on Willow pattern plate, together with printed m10. A similar mark has been found on a piece made by the Middlesboro' Pottery Company, but with the figure '18'. Possibly the Anchor mark belonged to a London retailer, and the different numbers refer to the factories of origin. (See m22.)

BELL, COOK & Co.

M12 Impressed mark occurring on one of a pair of jugs. Both also have the printed mark m13. [A blue Wild Rose plate and side plate (found while this work was in the press and consequently not illustrated) have similar M12 and m13 marks, but without the words NEWCASTLE-UPON-TYNE.] See p. 48.

m13 Printed mark on a pair of jugs, one together with M12. See p. 48.

BURN, Joseph, & Co.

M14 Impressed mark on a Willow pattern side plate, together with printed mark m15; thus identifying the latter, which occurs alone on several Willow pattern pieces in the author's collection.

m15 Printed mark of Burn & Co. Compare with Fell's marks m41, m42, m43. Burn appears to have tried to pass his wares off as those of the leading Tyneside firm of the day. See also p. 50.

CARR, John, and Co.

M16 Impressed mark on Tonquin pattern plate with printed mark m20. (M.B.)

m17 Printed mark on Willow pattern plate, together with impressed mark M21. (M.B.)

m18 Printed mark on a Willow pattern plate. (M.B.)

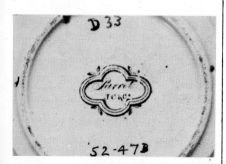

m19 Printed mark on cup and saucer, showing a woman in maroon with a parrot. Together with impressed mark M25. (L.A.G.)

m20 Printed mark on six Tonquin pattern plates by John Carr & Co., together with impressed mark M16. (M.B.)

CARR and Son

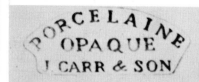

M21 Impressed mark on Willow pattern plate, together with printed mark m17.

m22 Printed mark on a Willow pattern side plate with impressed mark similar to M11, but without the number.

CARR, John, and Sons

M23 Impressed mark on Asiatic Pheasant side plate, together with printed mark m24. See p. 51.

m24 Printed mark on Asiatic Pheasant side plate, together with impressed mark M23.

M25 Impressed mark found alone, and also together with m26 on a blue and white geometric design, see p. 52, and on a Willow pattern side plate with m27. This shows that the 'Warranted Staffordshire' was made on Tyneside, and that John Carr & Sons used 'JC & Co', probably intending it to be mistaken for Joseph Clementson of Hanley.

m26 Printed mark on blue and white geometric design plate, together with impressed mark M25. See p. 148.

m27 Printed mark on Willow pattern side plate together with M25.

? CLEMENTSON, Joseph

m28 Printed mark on Willow pattern side plate. This is probably Joseph Clementson of the Phoenix Works, Shelton, Hanley (1839–64), but it may be another misleading mark of the North Shields firm of John Carr (see M25).

COLLINGWOOD & BEALL

m29 Printed mark on the side of a lustre-ware jug. See p. 18. (L.A.G.)

DAVIES, R., & Co.

M30 Impressed mark on 'Gaudy Welsh' plate. See p. 55. Also on a Willow pattern fish strainer.

M31 Impressed mark on the back of a tile. See p. 55.

DURHAM CHINA Co.

m32 Printed mark on Elizabeth II coronation mugs and beakers, and three flower pattern plates.

FELL, T., & Co.

M33 Impressed mark on the saucer of a cup and saucer showing two people having tea in a garden. (L.A.G.)

M34 Impressed mark on a fruit service of cream-ware with polychrome flowers with green borders. (L.A.G.)

M35 Impressed on the side of the base of a pot-pourri jar. See p. 61. (L.A.G.)

M36 Impressed mark on a bowl dated 28th June 1829. See p. 56. Also on a dragon pattern plate together with printed mark m40. (L.A.G.)

M37 Impressed mark on Wild Rose plate, together with printed mark m45. (L.A.G.)

M38 Impressed mark on a plate decorated in blue with a church ruin, a youth in a punt and a maiden playing a harp beneath a tree.

M39 Impressed mark on a small blue plate showing the Crown Prince of Sweden. (L.A.G.)

m40 Printed mark on a plate together with impressed mark M36. (L.A.G.)

m41 Printed mark on Willow pattern side plate together with impressed mark M33.

m42 Printed mark on Willow pattern plate.

m43 Printed mark on square Willow pattern fruit bowl, together with impressed mark M37.

m44 Printed mark on Wild Rose plate together with impressed mark M37.

m45 Printed mark on Wild Rose plate together with impressed mark M37. (L.A.G.)

m46 Printed mark on a pale blue basket with a Bosphorus design, together with M37. (L.A.G.)

m47 Printed mark on six commemorative plates decorated with portraits of the King and Queen of Greece (1867), together with mark M37.

m48 Printed mark on a plate decorated with a cowboy scene. (L.A.G.)

m49 Printed mark on Corinth pattern plate together with impressed mark M37, and a registration mark, 1845. (L.A.G.)

m50 Printed mark on a Willow pattern side plate, together with impressed mark M37.

m51 Printed mark on a jug decorated with a bramble design.

m52 Printed mark on hand-painted Renforth jug, and a transfer printed Shakespeare jug. See pp. 36 and 63.

FORDY, PATTERSON & Co.

M53 Impressed mark on small Willow pattern side plate, and a pink lustre cottage scene comfit plate; the latter. (L.A.G.)

GALLOWAY & ATKINSON

M54 Impressed mark on Willow pattern plates together with and without the printed mark of Isaac Bell, Galloway, Atkinson & Co., m9.

JACKSON & PATTERSON

J.&P
5

M55 Impressed mark on a small plate with flowers and leaves in blue and green enamel, and copper lustre on a field of purple lustre. (S.A.G.)

MALING, C. T.

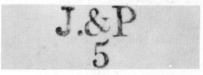

M56 Impressed mark on Willow pattern side plate together with printed mark m95 belonging to Robert Maling. This piece was probably made about 1853 when C. T. Maling took over from his father.

MALING

M57 Impressed mark on Willow pattern

plate. Probably a C. T. Maling mark, but may have been used by his father, Robert.

M58 Impressed mark first used about 1875 and continued by C. T. Maling & Sons until about 1908.

M59 Impressed mark on stone-ware marmalade jar (½ normal size).

M60 Impressed mark on a white-ware feeding cup, made about 1900.

m61 Printed mark on Willow pattern plate together with impressed mark M56.

m62 Printed mark on Willow pattern plate.

m63 Printed mark on Willow pattern plate with impressed mark '6.82', which indicated the date June 1882.

m64 Printed mark on two breakfast bowls printed in black; together with impressed mark M56.

p65 Painted mark on one of a pair of vases made for an exhibition in London in 1881. See p. 135.

m66 Printed mark on a sauce boat, transfer printed in green.

m67 Printed mark on a small oval dish decorated with the Brosley pattern in light blue, together with an impressed mark 'SS 6.87' which indicated a date of June 1887.

m68 Printed mark on a Willow pattern plate, together with impressed mark M58, and impressed date mark which is illegible.

MALING, C. T., & Sons

m69 Printed mark on a Diamond Jubilee mug (1897). See p. 89. (L.A.G.)

m70 Printed mark on overglaze printed French porcelain. See p. 150.

m71 Printed mark in use about 1908–20. This particular mark includes the name of the design, 'MOSS'. See p. 87.

m72 Printed mark on a coronation beaker of 1911. See p. 90.

m73 Printed marks, one in gold and one in blue, on a polychrome bowl with a crane design. See p. 118.

m74 Printed mark on a vegetable dish with an abstract pattern in blue and white.

m75 Printed mark on a basin with abstract blue printed border.

m76 Printed mark on souvenir mug of World War I. This mark was used on many second-quality pieces. See p. 89.

m77 Printed mark on a biscuit jar, red apples on blue background. See p.118.

m78 Printed mark on a meat dish with palmette and lotus border.

m79 Printed mark on an ash tray marked NEWCASTLE ALES. See p.75.

m80 Printed mark on a cream jug decorated with a border of Japanese apple blossom and pagoda with tree.

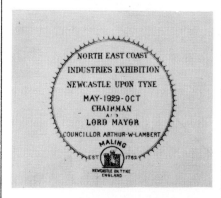

m81 Printed mark on commemorative plate of the North East Exhibition (1929). (Note 'EST 1762' on either side of the castle, a mark later used by Hoults during their period of ownership.)

m82 Printed mark on a mug showing the Tyne Bridge. Made for Watsons toffee manufacturers.

m83 Printed mark on a flower vase decorated with pansies. These were sold filled with tea c. 1935. See p.78.

m84 Printed mark on a blue transfer printed tea jar. The building is the headquarters of Ringtons Tea Co., Algernon Road, Heaton. See p.17.

m85 Printed mark on a red mug, a copy of 'Poor Richard's rise to fame'. (L.A.G.)

m86 Printed marks, black and gold superimposed on a bowl with polychrome decoration over black. See p. 8.

m87 Printed mark on polychrome lustre box with lilies. See p.118.

m88 Printed mark on cheaper wares produced during the Hoult ownership of C. T. Maling & Sons.

MALING, C. T., & Sons (Hoults)

m89 Printed mark on a giant teapot. See p. 79.

m90 Printed mark on a small bowl with peony rose design. See p. 94.

MALING, John

M91 Impressed mark on Willow pattern side plate. Provisionally ascribed to John Maling. See p.96.

MALING, Robert

M92 Impressed mark on Albion pattern side plate. See p.96.

M93 Impressed mark on pink exotic bird and flower comfit plate, together with printed mark m94. See p.97.

m94 Printed mark on pink exotic bird and flower comfit plate, together with impressed mark M93. See p.97

m95 Printed mark on Willow pattern side plate together with impressed mark M56 belonging to C. T. Maling. This piece was probably made about 1853 when Robert Maling resigned in favour of his son. See p.97

PATTERSON, George

M96 Impressed mark on four saucers in a child's tea set. The rest of the pieces are unmarked. See p. 99. Also on two Willow pattern tureens; and on a Grecian pattern side plate, together with printed mark m98. (S.A.G.)

G PATTERSON
GATESHEAD ON TYNE
14

M97 Impressed mark on an Albion pattern side plate, together with printed mark m100 (S.A.G.)

m98 Printed mark on Grecian pattern side plate, together with impressed mark M96. (S.A.G.)

m99 Printed mark on Willow pattern side plate. (S.A.G.)

m100 Printed mark on Albion pattern side plate, together with impressed mark M97. (S.A.G.)

m101 Printed mark on Willow pattern plate.

PATTERSON, Thomas
(Tyne Pottery)

M102 Impressed mark on pink cottage design lustre-ware. Also on a Willow pattern plate. See p. 100. (L.A.G.)

M103 Impressed mark on Willow pattern side plate, provisionally ascribed to Thomas Patterson after his move to Sheriff Hill. See p.101

PHOENIX POTTERY Co.

PHOENIX N'CASTLE

M104 Impressed mark on Willow pattern side plate. See p.102.

PRUDHOE POTTERY

p105 Painted mark on small wall decoration, one of three, only one being marked. See p.102

ROGERS, F.

ROGERS

M106 Impressed mark on Willow pattern side plate. See p.105

ST. ANTHONY'S POTTERY Co.

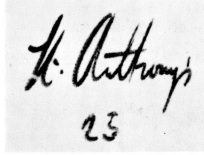

p107 Painted mark on a jug. See p. 105.

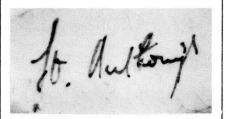

p108 Painted mark on leaf plate. See p.105

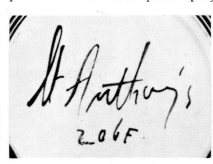

p109 Painted mark on a jug.

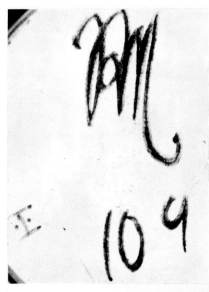

p110 Painted mark on a jug.

p111 Painted mark on vase. (This was the personal mark of Mr. Nixon.) See p.105.

SEWELL, Joseph

S ANTHONY

M112 Impressed mark on a cream-ware plate with a filigree edge. See p. 106. This mark is usually attributed to Joseph Sewell, though the present author believes it may have been used by one of the proprietors of St Anthony's before Sewell took over in 1804.

SEWELL

M113 Impressed mark on a blue and white castle design side plate. See p. 106.

SEWELL

M114 Impressed mark on cream-ware jug with green transfer printed design, dated 1845. At this date the firm was Sewell and Donkin, and an obsolete stamp must have been used, or old biscuit-ware decorated. The date on the vase on p. 136 is also at variance with the mark. See p.107. (L.A.G.)

SEWELL & DONKIN

M115 Impressed mark on a large round Willow pattern plate. See p. 108.

M116 Impressed mark on a black printed saucer. See p. 108.

M117 Impressed mark on cream-ware tureen and cover with hand painted floral decoration. (L.A.G.)

SEWELL & Co.

M118 Impressed mark on filigree cream-ware basket and stand. See p. 16. (L.A.G.)

TURNBULL

M119 Impressed mark on Albion pattern side plate. See p.110. (L.A.G.)

WALLACE & Co.

M120 Impressed mark on a Willow pattern side plate, together with printed mark 'opaque china'. (Not illustrated.) See p.111

m121 Printed mark on an Albion design plate. (S.A.G.)

m122 Printed mark on a Willow pattern plate.

WALLACE, James, & Co.

m123 Printed mark on a Willow pattern plate, together with an impressed anchor. It is possible that this piece may have been made by J. Wileman & Co., Foley China Works, Fenton, Staffordshire (1864–9), though the anchor was a popular device on Tyneside.

m124 Printed mark on a burial mug dated 1857 (the last year of the James Wallace & Co. firm). See p.112.

WILSON, R. C.

M125 Impressed mark on black transfer plate 'A present for William'. Provisionally attributed to R. C. Wilson.

WOOD, John

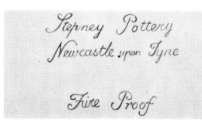

M126 Impressed mark found together with printed marks m128 and m130. See pp. 114-5.

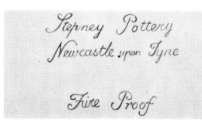

M127 Impressed mark on brown slip-ware pie dish. See p. 116.

m128 Printed mark together with impressed mark M126 on an Albion-design side plate. (L.A.G.)

m129 Printed mark together with impressed mark M126 on a side plate (p. 115). 'TYNE' refers to Tyneside, and not to a particular design.

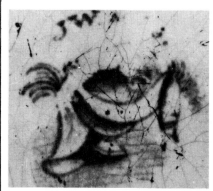

m130 Printed mark, together with impressed mark M126, on Albion pattern vegetable dish. See p. 114. (L.A.G.)

146

Bibliography

Anonymous, *An Account of Newcastle upon Tyne, 1787. An Alphabetical List of the people in Trade and their residence in Newcastle.*

Ball, W. R., 'Potteries of Sunderland and Neighbourhood', in *Antiquities of Sunderland*, vol. VII, 1906.

Buckley, F., 'Potteries on the Tyne, and other Northern Potteries during the Eighteenth Century', in *Archaeologia Aeliana, Fourth Series*, 1927, pp. 68–82.

Chaffers, William, *Marks and Monograms on European and Oriental Pottery and Porcelain*, 3rd edition, 1891.

Evans, W., *Art and History of the Potting Business*, 1846.

Fisher, S. W., *British Pottery and Porcelain*, London, Arco, 1962.

Godden, G. A., *Encyclopaedia of British Pottery and Porcelain Marks*, London, Herbert Jenkins, 1964.

Godden, G. A., *An Illustrated Encyclopaedia of British Pottery and Porcelain*, London, Herbert Jenkins, 1966.

Godden, G. A., *Handbook of British Pottery and Porcelain Marks*, London, Herbert Jenkins, 1968.

Haggar, R. G., *English Country Pottery*, London, Phoenix House, 1950.

Hodgson, G. B., *Borough of South Shields from the earliest period to the close of the nineteenth century*, Newcastle upon Tyne, Andrew Reid and Co., 1903, p. 408.

Honey, W. B., *English Pottery and Porcelain*, London, Black, 3rd edition, 1948.

Hughes, B. and T., *The Collectors Encyclopaedia of English Ceramics*, London, Lutterworth Press, 1956, p. 116.

Jewitt, L., *Ceramic Art of Great Britain*, 1878, vol. II, pp. 301–9.

Lewis, Griselda, *An Introduction to English Pottery*, London, Art and Technics Ltd., 1950.

Litchfield, F., *Pottery and Porcelain*, London, Truslove and Hanson, 2nd edition, 1905.

Maling, C. T., *The Industrial Resources of the District of the Three Northern Rivers, The Tyne, Wear, and Tees*, 2nd edition, 1864.

Mankowitz, W., and Haggar, R. G., *The Concise Encyclopedia of English Pottery and Porcelain*, London, André Deutsch, 1957, pp. 264–6.

Pottery Gazette and Glass Trade Review, June 1952.

Shaw, J. T., *The Potteries of Sunderland and District*, Sunderland, Public Libraries, Museum and Art Gallery, 3rd edition, 1968.

List of Directories

The following, mostly available in the Newcastle Central Library, were consulted. They vary considerably in quality and in the ease with which information can be extracted from them. Inclusion of a directory below does not mean that all the information contained in it has been utilised; some are tedious and difficult to use, and important material may have been overlooked.

1778	William Whitehead, *Newcastle Directory*
1782–4	*Newcastle and Gateshead Directory*
1801	J. Mitchell, *Directory of Newcastle and Gateshead*
1811	Mackenzie and Dent's *Triennial Directory for Newcastle and Gateshead*
1821–3	*Commercial Directory of Ireland, Scotland and Northern Counties of England*, 2nd edition
1824	*Directory for Newcastle upon Tyne and Gateshead*
1827–8	W. Parson and W. White, *History, Directory and Gazette of the Counties of Durham and Northumberland*, vol. 1 and vol. 2
1829	Pigot and Co's *New Commercial Directory*
1833	Alexander Ihler, *A directory of the towns of Newcastle and Gateshead and their Suburbs*
1834	Pigot and Co's *National Directory*
1837	Pigot and Co's *Directory of Scotland*. Appendix: 'Earthenware manufacturers, Newcastle'
1838	M. A. Richardson, *Directory of the towns of Newcastle and Gateshead*
1841	Robson's *Commercial Directory of Durham*
1844	Williams' *Commercial Directory of Newcastle upon Tyne, North and South Shields, etc.*
1847	Francis White and Co's *Directory of Newcastle, Gateshead, North and South Shields*
1850	Ward's *Northumberland and Durham Directory*
1851	Ward's *North of England Directory*
1852	Slater's *Royal National Commercial Directory & Topography of Scotland, etc., & Newcastle upon Tyne*
1853	Ward's *North of England Directory*
1855	*Post Office Directory of Northumberland and Durham* (Kelly and Co.)
	Slater's *Directory of the Northern Counties*, vol. 1
	Ward's *North of England Directory*
1857–62	Ward's *North of England Directory*
1863–4	Ward's *Directory of Newcastle and Gateshead*
1865–8	Ward's *Directory of Newcastle, Gateshead & Shields*
1869–70	Ward's *Directory of Newcastle, Gateshead, Sunderland*
1870–1	*The Newcastle and Gateshead Annual Directory*
1871–2	Ward's *Directory for Newcastle, Gateshead, Shields and Jarrow*
1873–4	Christies' *Newcastle and Gateshead Directory*
	Ward's *Directory of Newcastle, Gateshead and Sunderland*
1874–5	Christies' *Directory of Newcastle and Gateshead*
1877	Slater's *Directory of Northumberland, Durham, etc.*
1877–8	Ward's *Directory of Newcastle, Gateshead and Sunderland*
1878–80	Ward's *Directory of Newcastle, Gateshead, North and South Shields, etc.*
1879	Slater's *Directory of Cumberland, Durham, Northumberland and Westmorland*
	Post Office Directory of Durham & Northumberland
1880	Jackson's *Directory of Newcastle-on-Tyne & Tyneside*
1881–2	Ward's *Directory of Newcastle, Gateshead, North and South Shields, Jarrow and Sunderland*
1883	Kelley's *Directory of Newcastle, Gateshead, Sunderland, North and South Shields*
1883–4	Ward's *Directory of Newcastle, Gateshead, North and South Shields, Jarrow and Sunderland*
1884	Slater's *Directory of Durham and Northumberland*
1887	Bulmer's *Directory of Northumberland, Tyneside Division*
1887–8	Ward's *Directory of North and South Shields, Sunderland, Newcastle and Gateshead*
1888	Ward's *Directory of Newcastle on Tyne*
1889–90	Ward's *Directory of Newcastle, Gateshead, North and South Shields, Jarrow and Sunderland*
1890	Kelley's *Directory of Durham and Northumberland*
	Ward's *Directory of Newcastle upon Tyne*
1891–1904	Ward's *Directories of Newcastle, Gateshead, North and South Shields, etc.*
1892	Ward's *Directory of Newcastle on Tyne*
1894	Kelley's *Directory of Northumberland*
1898	Ward's *Directory of Newcastle on Tyne*
1899	Ward's *Directory of Newcastle on Tyne*
1902	Ward's *Directory of Newcastle and Wallsend*
1904	Ward's *Directory of Newcastle and Wallsend*
1905–6	Ward's *Directory of Newcastle and Gateshead*
1906	Ward's *Directory of Northumberland*
1907–28	Ward's *Directories of Newcastle upon Tyne*
1914	Kelley's *Directory of Northumberland and Durham*
1921	Kelley's *Directory of Northumberland*
1925	Kelley's *Directory of Northumberland*
1929	Kelley's *Directory of Northumberland*
1950–1	Kelley's *Directories of Newcastle on Tyne*

Addenda

Above left
One of six cockle plates marked, M 34.

Above right
Printed plate showing High and Low Level
Bridges at Newcastle.

While this work was in the press, the author found the following interesting items:
a) Six small cockle plates in perfect condition, black printed with pink lustre edges, and bearing the impressed mark of Fell, M 34. A reminder of the popularity of cockles as a delicacy in the early 19th century.
b) A black printed plate showing the High Level and Low Level Bridges across the Tyne at Newcastle, and bearing the printed mark of Townsend the China Dealer in Newcastle, with the impressed mark WEDGWOOD. Had the impressed mark been blurred, this could well confuse the collector into believing the piece to be of Tyneside origin (see pp. 23 and 24). Note the mis-spelling of 'Newcastl' without the final 'e'.
c) A blue printed dish in classical design with the printed mark of J. Wood Stepney Pottery (m129), but with the impressed mark SEWELLS, suggesting that when Sewell and Co. ceased production, part at least of their stock of biscuit-ware passed into the hands of John Wood, who then printed it with his own designs (see pp. 114-5).
d) A set of teapot, cream jug, sugar basin, and six cups and saucers marked with m 70, but made of fine white porcelain (see p. 150). Fortunately, one saucer explained this ceramic puzzle. The British firm had imported white chinaware from Limoges, France, decorated it with overglaze designs and gilt, and placed their own printed mark over that of the French factory, obliterating it whenever possible. This mark, m 70, may have been reserved for porcelain pieces, an explanation of its comparative rarity.

Below left
Impressed and printed marks on the printed plate illustrated above.

Below right
Blue printed dish marked M 118 and m 129.

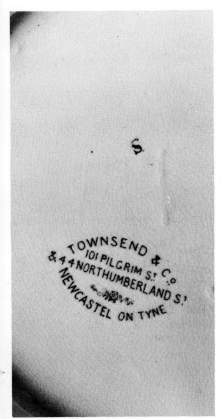

Cup and saucer of white porcelain decorated with overglaze designs and gilt.

Below left
Printed mark m 70, with traces of something beneath.

Below right
Printed mark m 70 on the bottom of a saucer, but with the original printed mark clearly visible, LIMOGES FRANCE.

Index

Numbers in **bold** indicate a main reference; in roman a minor reference; in *italic* an illustration.